VAUGHAN'S VEGETABLE COOK BOOK

LECTOR HOUSE PUBLIC DOMAIN WORKS

VAUGHAN'S VEGETABLE COOK BOOK

ANONYMOUS

ISBN: 978-93-89659-16-0

Published: 1919

VAUGHAN'S VEGETABLE COOK BOOK

HOW TO COOK AND USE
RARER VEGETABLES AND HERBS

A BOON TO HOUSEWIVES

FOURTH EDITION

1919

FRENCH ENDIVE OR WITLOOF CHICORY

A WHOLESOME AND USEFUL WINTER VEGETABLE

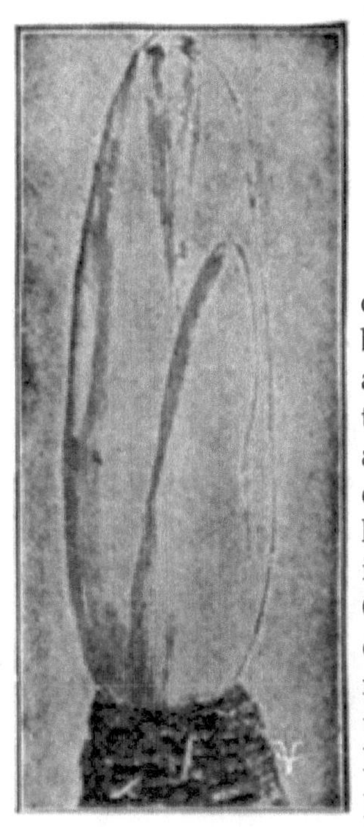

How to Grow. Sow the seed in Spring on well prepared land 1 ft. apart in rows, and thin out same as parsnips. Lift the roots in fall. These roots produce during winter months, the beautiful young crisp leaves, which make one of the most delicious winter salads. Here's how it's done.

Forcing the Roots. Prepare a convenient sized bed of good rich soil about a foot deep, in the basement and board up the sides. Place the roots in it until the crowns are just covered, and about 2 inches apart, in rows 6 to 8 inches apart then place on top about 8 inches of any kind of light covering such as leaf mold or other light compost. This **must be light** or otherwise the heads which will grow from the crown will open out instead of keeping firmly closed and conically shaped. On the top of the light soil, manure (if it can be procured fresh, all the better) should be placed to a thickness of about 12 inches, or even more. This will cause the soil to warm slightly and hasten the making of the head. Horse manure is better than cattle manure for the purpose. The heads will be ready to cut in from 4 to 6 weeks. By putting in a batch at 10 day intervals, a succession of cuttings may be made from the bed. Store the roots in dry sand until they are to be put in the bed.

Roots may also be forced in a Greenhouse or Conservatory by planting under the benches or in a specially prepared place, but not too high a temperature; say anywhere from 55 to 60 degrees F. To give more is running the risk of getting spindly, weak heads. They may also be grown in pots of say 12 inch drain. Place from five to six roots in a pot, leaving the crown of the root exposed and place another pot inverted closely over it, covering up the top hole, so as to keep the roots as dark as possible. Water about once a day and in a temperature of from 55 to 65 degrees. It will take about one month, or even less before the heads may be cut. After cutting they must be kept dark, else they turn green quickly. The roots after being forced, indoors or outdoors, become useless.

Use. The leaves can be used in every way that lettuce can, and are delicious either alone, or in combination salads. It is beautifully crisp, tender and has a delightful appetizing flavor of its own. Large quantities are imported into this country from Europe every year and it is found on the bill of fare of all First Class Restaurants during the winter months.

Grown at home (and so easily grown at that) and served fresh and crisp from the bed, its true qualities are doubly appreciated.

PREFACE

THIRD EDITION

THE suggestions and recipes of this cook book have been gathering through the years from sources far and wide. Friends and neighbors have contributed, personal experience has offered its lessons, thrifty housekeepers in home departments of newspapers, reports of lectures, and recipes given to the newspaper world, from teachers in the science of cookery, have all added color or substance to what is herein written. The recipes of the CHICAGO RECORD-HERALD, rich in material, have been drawn on to a limited extent, credit is given to an owner of a recipe if known, if not it is given to the paper. Compound recipes have been made up from the study of several cook books. "The Cook's Own Book," "The Household," "Practical Housekeeping." French and German recipes have all in some degree been a source of supply to this compilation. We offer the result to you, hoping it will fill a need, and though a wee thing among its grown up sisters, that it will find a place, all its own, in your esteem and good will.

The demand which has made a Third Edition now necessary is the best proof that the volume has found favor, and the ever increasing love of gardening finds its definite expression in this direction as in many other new ones.

Chicago, January 9th, 1919

CONTENTS

CONTENTS ix

CHINESE CABBAGE—PE TSAI

A few years ago this delicious vegetable was introduced into this country, though it has been well known and extensively cultivated in China for a long time.

We have grown it at our trial grounds two seasons and have found it a novel, easily grown delicious vegetable. In shape it resembles a giant cos lettuce forming a head some fifteen inches long.

When nearing maturity the outer leaves should be tied up to blanch the heart and when cut two weeks later and the outer leaves removed, appears as a grand oblong solid white head, of crisp tender leaves. We have noticed that late sowing i. e. July gives the largest and best heads. Sown earlier it runs to seed.

Plant in rows 1 ft. apart, with 2 1/2 or 3 ft. between the rows. Water and cultivate freely. For Winter use store same as cabbage, keep from freezing.

Uses. The heads may be cut into convenient sizes and served like lettuce, but is we think, more delicious, when cooked like cabbage and served up in any of the many ways that cabbage is.

SEA KALE

An easily grown vegetable, especially valuable when forced during the winter months.

To raise from seed sow in April, lift the roots in Fall and plant out the following Spring in rows 2 ft. apart.

Sea Kale needs well dug, well manured soil and plenty of water. We recommend planting roots (3 year old preferably). Cover the bed with light blanching material, 7 or 8 ins. deep and cut same as Asparagus (Coal ashes is what is usually used for Seakale). It should be ready to cut in 6 or 8 weeks. To get it early, plant 3 roots in hills 4 ft. apart. Place an old bucket or box over the hill and cover all over with fresh stable manure. The heat from the manure will make cutting possible in 2 or 3 weeks; 4 or 6 buckets or boxes may be used and transferred to other hills when first hills are through. (Roots can be procured in the Fall.)

Forcing Inside. Plant 3 to 5 roots in an 8 in. pot and invert a similar pot over it and cover the hole in the top. Place under bench in conservatory or Greenhouse, or in a warm basement where 50 or 60 degrees may be maintained. Water every day. Cutting should be made in from 18 to 21 days, according to heat maintained.

Use. Seakale is considered a great delicacy, the young shoots when cooked are more tender than the youngest Asparagus. They are usually cooked whole and served with white (cream) sauce as Asparagus, or may be chopped up and cooked like celery and served in the same manner. It has a nice buttery flavor of its own, that has to be tasted to be appreciated, a flavor that will take with the household. We do not hesitate to say that if once grown the demand will soon exceed the supply.

VAUGHAN'S VEGETABLE COOK BOOK

INTRODUCTION

Vegetables are at their best in their own season, just as nature develops them, not as man forces them. Gathered not quite full grown with the dew of the morning upon them, they are solid, tender, juicy, sweet and full of flavor, fit for a feast of the gods. But the crispness, sweetness and fresh flavors are fleeting, and few but owners of, and neighbors to gardens know the prime flavors of the fruits and vegetables upon their tables.

Therefore in selecting vegetables for your table choose first the freshest possible, select medium sized and not overgrown ones, though small sized turnips and large rutabagas are best, egg-plants should be full grown, but not ripe. If vegetables are not fresh refresh them by plunging them into cold salt water an hour before cooking. Old potatoes should be pared as thin as possible and be thrown at once into cold salt water for several hours, changing the water once or twice. Wipe plunged vegetables before cooking. Old potatoes are improved by paring before baking. Irish or sweet potatoes, if frozen, must be put into bake without thawing. Onions should be soaked in warm salt water an hour before cooking to modify their rank flavor. Lettuce, greens, and celery are sometimes best cleaned by using warm water, though they must be thrown at once, when cleaned, into cold water. To steam vegetables is better than to boil them, their flavors are held better, they are less liable to be water-soaked and their odors are confined instead of escaping through the house. If they are to be boiled always draw fresh water. Mrs. Rorer says, "Soft water should be used for dry vegetables, such as split peas, lentils and beans, and hard water for green ones. Water is made soft by using a half teaspoonful of bi-carbonate of soda to a gallon of water, and hard by using one teaspoonful of salt to a gallon of water." As soon as the water boils, before it parts with its gases, put in the vegetables. Use open vessels except for spinach. The quicker they boil the better. As soon as tender, take them out of the water, drain and dress for the table. Never let them remain in the water after they are once done. Fresh vegetables boil in about 1/3 of the time of old ones. A little bi-carbonate of soda added to the boiling water before greens are put in will serve to keep their color. A pinch of pearl ash put into boiling peas will render old yellow ones, quite tender and green. A little sugar improves beets, turnips, peas, corn, squash, tomatoes and pumpkins, especially if they are not in prime condition. A little lime boiled in water improves very watery potatoes. A piece of red pepper the size of a finger nail, a small piece of charcoal or even a small piece of bread crust, dropped in with boiling vegetables will modify unpleasant odors. Vegetables served with salt meats must be boiled in the liquor of the meat after it has been boiled and removed. Egg-plant and old potatoes are often put on to cook in cold salt water. It is claimed that onions, carrots, and turnips cook quicker if cut in rings across the fiber. Clean all vegetables thoroughly to remove all dirt and insects. To free leaves from insects, throw vegetables, stalk ends uppermost, into a strong brine made by putting one and one half pounds of salt into a gallon of water. Leave them in the brine for two or three hours, and the insects will fall off and sink to the bottom.

BOILED ARTICHOKES.

The edible part of a French Artichoke is the base of the scales and the bottom of the artichoke. The Jerusalem artichoke is a genuine tuber something like a potato. They are differently treated in preparation for cooking, but are cooked similarly. To prepare a French artichoke for boiling, pull off the outer leaves, cut the stalks close to the bottom, wash well and throw into cold salt water for two hours. To boil, plunge them into boiling salted water, stalk end up with an inverted plate over them to keep them down. Boil until very tender, season well, drain and arrange on a dish with tops up. Pour over any good vegetable sauce. (See **Sauces**.) To prepare Jerusalem artichokes for boiling pare and slice thin into cold water to prevent turning dark, boil in salted water, season and serve with drawn butter or a good sauce.

CREAMED ARTICHOKES.

Slice six artichokes, boil in salted water and when tender, drain. Brown slightly in a saucepan one tablespoonful of butter and a dessert spoonful of flour, add a cup of rich milk, season with a half teaspoonful of salt, the same amount of sugar and a dash of pepper; boil two minutes, then stir in two eggs well beaten in two tablespoonfuls of milk, add the artichokes and the juice of half a lemon and let simmer three minutes longer; when dished up sprinkle one-third of a salt spoon of pepper over them and serve hot.

FRIED ARTICHOKES.

Boil and drain six artichokes, season with a sprinkling of vinegar, a little salt and pepper and stand them aside for an hour; beat an egg, add to it a tablespoonful of warm water, dip each slice in this, then in flour and fry in hot fat. Serve with Sauce Tartare. (See **Sauces**.)

Mrs. S. T. Rorer.

ARTICHOKES A LA LYONNAISE.

Boil, drain, put into a saucepan with melted butter and sweet oil and brown on both sides, season with salt. Add a half cupful of meat stock, thicken with a little flour and butter, and boil three minutes, squeeze a little lemon juice into it, add a sprinkling of parsley and a dash of pepper, pour over the artichokes and serve.

French Recipe.

PICKLED ARTICHOKES.

Parboil artichokes, and pour over good strong vinegar. They make excellent pickles.

ARTICHOKE SOUP.

Slice into cold water to keep the color, boil an hour or more in two quarts of water, season highly with butter, pepper and salt, and just before taking up, add a cup of cream.

ARTICHOKES A LA VINAIGRETTE.

Pare and throw into cold water at once. When ready for use cut into thin slices, arrange them on lettuce leaves and serve with a French dressing. (See **Salad Dressing**.)

AMBUSHED ASPARAGUS.

Use one quart of the tender tops of asparagus, and be rid of the white part, which will not cook tender, boil and drain. Cut off with care the tops from rolls or biscuits a day old, scoop out the inside, and set the shells and tops into the oven to crisp. Boil a pint of milk, and when boiled stir in four eggs well whipped. As it thickens season with a tablespoonful of butter; salt and pepper to taste. Into this mixture put the asparagus cut up into small pieces. Fill the shells, replace the tops, put into the oven for three minutes and serve very hot.

BAKED ASPARAGUS.

Choose the freshest asparagus possible, trim the tops, scrape or peel the stalks, cut them into equal lengths and tie into small bunches; boil in salted water, drain, cut into inch pieces and put into a buttered baking dish; pour over a white sauce, (See **Sauces**) cover the top with grated cheese and bread crumbs, and bake until a golden brown.

BOILED ASPARAGUS.

Prepare as for baked asparagus, and when boiled tender in salted water, pour over a drawn butter sauce; or prepare a sauce from the water drained from the asparagus by thickening with one tablespoonful of butter, one tablespoonful of flour and the beaten yolk of an egg, to which add seasoning and lemon or nutmeg to suit taste.

ESCALLOPED ASPARAGUS.

Make alternate layers of boiled asparagus, a sprinkling of chopped hard boiled eggs and a sprinkling of grated cheese until the baking pan is full, having asparagus the top layer. Make a well seasoned milk gravy and pour gradually into the pan that it may soak through to the bottom, cover the top with bread crumbs and a light sprinkle of cheese; bake until a light brown.

FRIED ASPARAGUS.

Parboil the asparagus, dip in egg, then in bread crumbs, or use a batter and fry in hot fat. Sprinkle with salt and serve.

ASPARAGUS WITH EGGS.

Put boiled asparagus into a heated baking dish, season well, break eggs over it and put into the oven until the eggs are set, or beat the yolks and whites of four eggs separately; mix with the yolks two tablespoonfuls of milk or cream, a heaping teaspoonful of butter, salt and pepper, and lastly the beaten whites of the eggs; pour all over the asparagus and bake until the eggs are set.

ASPARAGUS OMELET.

Make a plain omelet and when the eggs are firming, lay over one half of it hot seasoned tops of asparagus, and fold over the other half.

ASPARAGUS SALAD.

Drain boiled asparagus and set on ice until used. Make a bed of crisp tender lettuce leaves, lay on these slices of fresh solid tomatoes, and over these a layer of asparagus: pour over all a French or mayonnaise dressing. (See **Salad Dressing**.)

ASPARAGUS SOUP.

Boil tips and stalks separately, when the stalks are soft, mash and rub them through a sieve. Boil a pint of rich milk, thicken it with a tablespoonful each of butter and flour and add the water in which the asparagus was boiled and the pulp. Season with salt, pepper, a very little sugar, and lastly a gill of cream, add the tips, boil all together a minute and serve with toast or crackers.

STRING BEANS AND APPLES.

Take three parts of string beans to one part apples. Break the beans into small pieces, pare and quarter the apples. Boil the beans in salted water until soft, and drain. Mix a tablespoonful each of butter and flour in a saucepan, and add to this, three tablespoonfuls each of vinegar and water and season with salt. Pour over the beans and let cook until they are well seasoned. Boil the apples and add thin slices of lemon. When all is ready add the apples to the beans without too much juice. Serve either hot or cold.

GERMAN RECIPE.

FAVRE BEANS.

Beans and oysters form this dish. Cook the beans until tender and they must not be dry either. Put an inch thick layer of beans in a baking dish, sprinkle with salt, pepper and bits of butter, cover with a layer of raw oysters, then beans, seasoning and oysters again, and so continue until the dish is full. Sprinkle cracker dust or bread crumbs thickly over the top, strew over bits of butter and bake in a well heated oven three-quarters of an hour. Do not let the top get too deep a brown.

FRICASSEE OF BEANS.

Steep one pint of haricot beans for a night in cold water, then remove them, drain and put on the fire with two quarts of soft water. When boiling allow the beans to simmer for another two hours. While they are cooking thus, put on in another saucepan two ounces of butter, an ounce of parsley (chopped) and the juice of one lemon, and when the butter has quite melted throw in the beans and stir them round for a few minutes. To be served with rice.

HARICOT BEANS.

Soak a pint of beans over night, cook the next morning until perfectly soft, strain through a sieve and season with one teaspoonful of salt and a saltspoonful of pepper. From this point this mass is capable of many treatments. It is made into a plain loaf sprinkled with bread crumbs, dotted with butter and baked, or it is mixed with a cream sauce and treated the same way, or it is made into a plain croquet, dipped into batter and fried, or it is seasoned with a tablespoonful of molasses, vinegar and butter and made into croquets, or it is mixed with a French dressing and eaten while it is warm as a warm salad.

LIMA BEANS.

After shelling a quart of lima beans, cook in boiling salted water until tender, then stir in a lump of butter the size of an egg and pepper and salt to taste; or season with milk or cream, butter, salt and pepper, or melt a piece of butter the size of an egg, mix with it an even teaspoonful of flour, and a little meat broth to make a smooth sauce. Put the beans in the sauce and let them simmer very slowly for fifteen minutes. Just before serving add a tablespoonful of chopped parsley and salt and pepper to taste.

STRING BEANS BOILED.

Take the pods as fresh and young as possible and shred them as finely as a small knife will go through them, cutting them lengthwise. Put into salted water and boil until tender. Then drain and serve with plenty of sweet butter, and they will be as delicate as peas. If one likes vinegar, a little of it will improve the dish.

STRING BEANS PICKLED.

Boil beans until tender, and then put into strong vinegar; add green peppers to taste.

STRING BEAN SALAD.

Cook the beans in salted water, drain and season while warm with salt, pepper, oil and vinegar. A little onion juice is an improvement. (See **French Salad Dressing**.)

STRING BEAN SOUP.

Boil one pint of string beans cut in inch lengths, in one pint of veal or celery stock and one pint of water, add a few slices of potatoes, a stalk of tender celery chopped, half a small onion, two or three leaves of summer savory and a clove. When soft rub through a sieve. Put in a saucepan and cook together a tablespoonful of butter, a heaping tablespoonful of flour and a pint of rich milk. Add this to the stock and pulp, season with pepper and salt and serve.

WHITE NAVY BEANS CURRIED.

If the fresh kidney beans are not obtainable soak a pint of the dried over night. Boil in two quarts of water for two hours or until tender. Drain, when soft, and put into a saucepan with an ounce of butter, one small onion chopped fine, one saltspoonful of salt and a half-teaspoonful of curry powder. Toss the beans in this mixture for a few moments over the fire; then mix smoothly a tablespoonful of flour with a large cup of milk and season highly with a tablespoonful each of chopped parsley, chopped bacon, tomato catchup and chutney, adding also a saltspoonful of salt, and add to the beans; set the saucepan on the back of the range and let the contents simmer three-quarters of an hour, adding more milk if the curry becomes too thick. Serve with plain boiled rice.

CHICAGO RECORD.

BAKED BEETS.

Bake two large beets, take off the hard outside, and the inner part will be surprisingly sweet. Slice and pour over a sauce made with two tablespoonfuls of butter, juice of half a lemon, a half teaspoonful of salt and a dash of pepper.

BEETS AND BUTTER SAUCE.

Boil three or four beets until tender in fast boiling water, slightly salted, which must entirely cover them. Then scrape off the skin, cut the beets into slices, and the slices into strips. Melt an ounce of butter, add to it a little salt, pepper, sugar and a teaspoonful of vinegar. Pour over the beets and serve. A small minced onion added to the sauce is sometimes considered an improvement.

BEET SALAD.

Slice cold boiled beets; cut into neat strips, and serve with white crisp lettuce; pour over a mayonnaise dressing; or slice the beets and put in layers with slices of hard boiled eggs, or, with new potatoes and serve on lettuce with French dressing garnished with water cress.

SWEET PICKLED BEETS.

Boil beets in a porcelain kettle till they can be pierced with a silver fork; when cold cut lengthwise to size of a medium cucumber; boil equal parts of vinegar and sugar, with a half tablespoonful of ground cloves to a gallon of vinegar; pour boiling hot over the beets.

SUGAR BEET PUDDING.

The following recipe of Juliet Corson's was traveling the round of the newspapers a few years ago:—Boil the beets just tender, peel and cut into small dice. Take a pint of milk to a pint of beets, two or three eggs well beaten, a palatable seasoning of salt and pepper and the least grating of nutmeg; put these ingredients into an earthen dish that can be sent to the table; bake the pudding until the custard is set, and serve it hot as a vegetable. A favorite Carolina dish.

BOILED BORECOLE OR KALE.

Use a half peck of kale. Strip the leaves from the stems and choose the crisp and curly ones for use, wash through two waters and drain. Boil in salted water twenty minutes, then pour into a colander and let cold water run over it, drain and chop fine. Brown a small onion in a tablespoonful of butter, and add the kale, seasoning with salt and pepper, add a half teacupful of the water in which the kale was boiled, and let all simmer together for twenty minutes. Just before taking from the stove add a half cup of milk or cream, thickening with a little flour. Let boil a moment and serve.

KALE GREENS.

These make excellent greens for winter and spring use. Boil hard one half hour with salt pork or corned beef, then drain and serve in a hot dish. Garnish with slices of hard boiled eggs, or the yolks of eggs quirled by pressing through a patent potato masher. It is also palatable served with a French dressing.

KALE ON TOAST.

Boil kale, mix with a good cream sauce and serve on small squares of toast.

BROCCOLI.

Broccoli if not fresh is apt to be bitter in spite of good cooking. Strip off all the side shoots, leaving only the top; cut the stalk close to the bottom of the bunch, throw into cold water for half an hour, drain, tie in a piece of cheese cloth to keep it from breaking and boil twenty minutes in salted water. Take out carefully, place upon a hot dish, pour over it a cream sauce and serve very hot; or it may be served on toast.

BRUSSELS SPROUTS.

Wash in cold water, pick off the dead leaves, put them in two quarts of boiling water, with a tablespoonful of salt, and a quarter teaspoonful of bi-carbonate of soda. Boil rapidly for twenty minutes with the saucepan uncovered, then drain in a colander, and serve with drawn butter or a cream sauce.

BOILED CABBAGE.

Slice a cabbage fine and boil in half water and half milk, when tender add cream and butter. This is delicious.

A CABBAGE CENTER PIECE.

Take a head of cabbage, one that has been picked too late is best, for the leaves open better then, and are apt to be slightly curled. Lay the cabbage on a flat plate or salver and press the leaves down and open with your hand, firmly but gently, so as not to break them off. When they all lie out flat, stab the firm, yellow heart through several times with a sharp knife, until its outlines are lost and then place flowers at random all over the cabbage.

Roses are prettiest, but any flower which has a firm, stiff stem, capable of holding the blossom upright will do. Press the stems down through the leaves and put in sufficient green to vary prettily. The outer leaves of the cabbage, the only ones to be seen when the flowers are in, form a charming background, far prettier than any basket.

Roses are best for all seasons, but autumn offers some charming variations. The brilliant scarlet berries of the mountain ash or red thorn mingled with the deep, rich green of feathery asparagus, make a delicious color symphony most appropriate to the season.

G. L. COLBRON.

CREAM SLAW.

Chop a crisp head of cabbage fine, place in the individual dishes in which it is to be served; fill a cup with white sugar, moisten it with vinegar, add a cup of sour cream beaten until smooth, mix thoroughly, pour over the cabbage and serve at once.

CABBAGE A LA HOLLAND.

The following is a favorite dish in Holland:—Put together in a saucepan, either porcelain or a perfect granite one, a small head of red cabbage shredded, four tart apples peeled and sliced, one large tablespoonful of butter or of drippings, a teaspoonful of salt, a half teaspoonful of pepper, and a little sprinkling of cheese or nutmeg; stew over a slow fire at least three hours. Mix together one tablespoonful of vinegar, a little flour and one tablespoonful of currant jelly, just before taking from the fire add this mixture to the cabbage, boil up once or twice and serve.

RED CABBAGE PICKLE.

This is an improvement on saur kraut. Slice a large red cabbage in fine shreds, place on a large platter and sprinkle well with salt; allow it to stand three days and then drain. Heat enough vinegar to cover it nicely, and put in one ounce of whole spices, pepper, cloves, allspice and mace. Put the cabbage into a stone jar, pour the boiling vinegar upon it, cover and let stand three days.

CABBAGE PUDDING.

Chop up small, enough white cabbage to fill a large baking pan when done. Put it in a pot of boiling water that has been salted, let it boil until tender, then drain thoroughly in a colander. In two quarts of the cabbage stir half a pound of butter, salt and pepper to taste, one pint of sweet cream and four eggs beaten separately. Add also, a pinch of cayenne pepper; put in a pan and bake for half an hour.

PURITAN CABBAGE.

Take half of a small very solid head of white cabbage, cut into eighths, from top to stem, without cutting quite through the stem so that it does not fall into pieces; cover with cold water for one hour; then immerse it in a porcelain kettle of rapidly boiling water, into which has been dropped a teaspoonful of salt and soda the size of a pea. Cover the vessel well and continue boiling for five minutes; drain, cover again with fresh boiling water and let boil for eight or ten minutes longer. Take out of water, draining, flat side down, on a hot platter for a moment. Then turn right side up, allowing the slices to spread apart a little, and drop slowly over it the following sauce: One tablespoon butter and two tablespoons sweet cream, melted together. Select and have ready to use at once, eighteen or twenty plump, good sized oysters, tdried on a towel. Take a double-wire gridiron and butter it well; spread the oysters carefully on one side of the gridiron and fold the other side down over them. Have a clear fire and broil them quickly, first one side, then the other, turning iron but once. Dot them over the hot cabbage, giving all a faint dust of curry powder and two or three dashes of white pepper. This is a most dainty and delicious dish.

CHICAGO RECORD.

CABBAGE SALAD.

This salad requires about a pint and a half of chopped cabbage. The cabbage should have the loose leaves removed, the stem cut out, and then be laid in cold water twelve hours. Chop rather fine, pour over and mix with it a boiled dressing. Heat three-quarters of a cup of milk and beat two egg yolks with a fork. Mix with the egg a half-teaspoonful of mustard, one half-teaspoonful of salt, a teaspoonful of granulated gelatine that has been softened in a little cold water, a teaspoonful of sugar and a few grains of cayenne. Cook a tablespoonful of butter and flour together and add half a cup of vinegar. Now cook the milk and egg mixture together like a soft custard and combine with the other part. This dressing, if sealed tight, will keep a long time. When the cabbage and dressing are mixed, fill little individual molds and set away to cool. After-dinner coffee cups, wet in cold water, make good molds. Bits of red beet or half an olive put in the bottom of the mold before the cabbage is put in will make a pretty garnish when the salad is turned out.

CHICAGO RECORD.

SOUR CABBAGE.

Beat one half-cupful of sour cream until smooth, add three tablespoonfuls of vinegar, and one beaten egg, pour over chopped cabbage raw or boiled, and mix thoroughly. Serve on lettuce.

STUFFED CABBAGE.

Use a savoy cabbage, open up the leaves and wash thoroughly in cold water, put in salted boiling water and boil five minutes, then take out without breaking, and put in cold water. Make a stuffing of sausage meat, and bread crumbs which have been moistened and squeezed. To a half pound of sausage allow one egg, two tablespoonfuls of minced onion browned in butter, a pinch of parsley and four tablespoonfuls of minced cooked ham. Drain, and open up the cabbage to the center, between the leaves put in a half teaspoonful of the stuffing, fold over two or three leaves, put in again and so continue until the cabbage is filled. When finished press it as firmly as the case will allow, tie up in a piece of cheese cloth and put into boiling water; boil two hours. Serve the cabbage in a deep dish and pour over a cream sauce.

TURKISH CABBAGE.

Prepare the cabbage as above for stuffing, then cut out the stalk carefully. Cut each leaf in pieces about three inches square and fold into it a forcemeat of some sort, or a highly seasoned vegetable dressing. These little rolls are arranged in layers in a saucepan and are held in place by the weight of a heavy plate; a broth is then turned over them and they are boiled half an hour over a moderate fire. Serve in a hot deep dish and pour over a good sauce made from the broth in which they were cooked.

CARROTS A LA CREME.

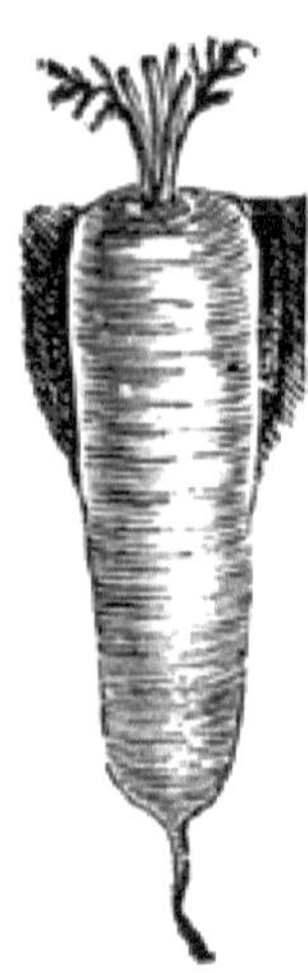

Take a large bunch of very small new carrots, scrape them, tie them loosely in a piece of coarse muslin and put into a saucepan almost full of boiling water, to which has been added a small lump of beef drippings and two ounces of salt. In about twenty minutes they will be tender, when remove from the hot water and plunge for a moment in cold. Next melt an ounce of butter in a saucepan and stir into this a dessert spoonful of flour, a small quantity each of pepper, salt and cayenne, also a little nutmeg and half a teacupful of cream. Remove the carrots from the muslin, put them into the saucepan with the other ingredients and let them simmer in them for a few minutes; then serve very quickly while hot. Green peas and carrots mixed and dressed in this way make an excellent variation.

CARROTS A LA FLAMANDE.

When par-boiled and drained, put the carrots into a saucepan with a piece of butter, a small lump of sugar and as much water as may be necessary for sauce; add some finely minced parsley and pepper and salt to the taste. Let the carrots simmer until done (about fifteen minutes) shaking them occasionally. Beat together the yolks of two eggs and two tablespoonfuls of cream; stir this into the carrots off the fire and serve.

CARROT CROQUETTES.

Wash six small, fine-grained carrots and boil until tender. Drain and mash them. To each cupful add one-half spoonful of salt and one-fourth as much pepper, the yolks of two raw eggs, a grate of nutmeg and one level teaspoonful of butter. Mix thoroughly and set away until cold. Shape into tiny croquettes, dip in slightly beaten egg, roll in fine bread crumbs and fry in smoking-hot fat.

CHICAGO RECORD.

FRIED CARROTS.

When the carrots are boiled tender, slice them lengthwise. Into a frying pan put one tablespoonful of butter, and when very hot put in the carrots; brown them lightly on both sides, sprinkle them with salt, pepper and a little sugar and garnish with parsley.

ESCALLOPED CARROTS.

Take six small fine-grained carrots and two small white onions, boil in water until tender, from forty-five to sixty minutes, just enough water to keep from burning. Do not scrape them, and the flavor will be retained; do not cover them and the color will be preserved. When the onions are tender remove them. When the carrots are done peel them and slice thin. Put in baking dish a layer of carrots, sprinkle with salt and pepper and dots of butter. Proceed in this way until you have used all the carrots. Moisten with a cup of new milk, into which a beaten egg has been carefully stirred, and a good pinch of salt. Spread over the top a layer of bread crumbs and bake until a nice brown.

CHICAGO RECORD.

PRESERVED CARROTS.

Scrape carrots clean, cut into small pieces and boil with sufficient cold water to cover them. Boil until tender, and put through the colander, weigh the carrots, add white sugar pound for pound and boil five minutes. Take off and cool. When cool add the juice of two lemons and the grated rind of one, two tablespoonfuls of brandy and eight or ten bitter almonds chopped fine to one pound of carrot. Stir all in well and put in jars.

CARROT SOUP.

Boil a pint of carrots with a piece of butter about as large as a walnut and a lump of sugar until they are tender. Press through a colander and put into a pint of boiling milk, thickened with a tablespoonful each of butter and flour, dilute this with soup stock or chicken broth, and just before taking up add the yolks of two eggs well beaten and two tablespoonfuls of cream.

BAKED CAULIFLOWER.

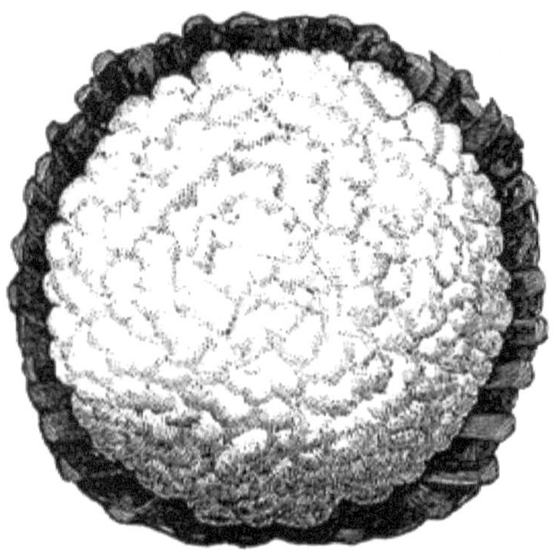

Boil cauliflower in salt water, separate into small pieces, and put in a baking dish, make a cream sauce and pour over it. Cover the mixture with bread crumbs, dot with butter and bake a light brown.

BOILED CAULIFLOWER WITH WHITE SAUCE.

Cut off the stem close to the bottom of the flower and pick off the outer leaves. Wash well in cold water and let it lie in salt and water top downward for an hour to remove any insects which may be in the leaves. Then tie in a cheese cloth or salt bag to prevent its going to pieces, and put, stem downward, in a kettle of boiling water with a teaspoonful of salt. Cover and boil till tender, about half an hour. Lift it out carefully, remove the cloth and arrange, stem downward, in a round, shallow dish. Pour over it a cream sauce.

FRIED CAULIFLOWER.

Take cauliflower cooked the day before, divide into small tufts, dip in egg and roll in cracker or bread crumbs, or make a batter in the proportion of one egg, two tablespoonfuls of milk and one tablespoonful of flour. Beat the eggs very light before adding to the milk and flour, and into this dip the cauliflower. Have the butter boiling hot in the frying pan, put in the cauliflower and fry a light brown, garnish with parsley.

PICKLED CAULIFLOWER.

Boil the cauliflower not too soft and break up into small tufts. Drain and put into bottles with horse-radish, tarragon, bay leaves and grains of black pepper. Pour over good cider vinegar and cork the bottle tightly.

CAULIFLOWER SALAD.

This salad is what Mrs. Rorer terms delicious served with her favorite French dressing. Take a head of cauliflower and boil in a piece of fine cheesecloth. Remove from the cloth, drain and sprinkle over it two tablespoons of lemon juice or vinegar and stand aside to cool. At serving time break the head apart into flowerets, arrange them neatly on a dish; sprinkle over a little chopped parsley or the wild sorrel; cover with French dressing made as follows; put a half-teaspoon of salt and as much white pepper into a bowl; add gradually six tablespoons of olive oil. Rub until the salt is dissolved, and then add one tablespoon of vinegar or lemon juice. Beat well for a moment and it is ready to use. It is much better if used at once.

CAULIFLOWER SOUP.

Boil a head of cauliflower in water, or if convenient in soup stock or chicken broth. If water is used add an onion. Lift out the cauliflower, lay aside one half-pint of tufts. Mash the rest through a sieve using the water in which it was boiled to press it through. Put one large tablespoonful of butter over the fire in a saucepan and when melted stir in a large tablespoon of flour. Stir this into the puree until of a creamy consistency, add a pint of hot milk, a beaten egg, salt and pepper to taste and a little grated nutmeg if liked. Add the reserved tufts, simmer five minutes and serve.

CAULIFLOWER AND TOMATO SOUFFLE.

Boil cauliflower in salted water until tender, then drain and separate into tufts. Put in a buttered baking dish a layer of tufts, then a layer of tomatoes, salt and pepper the tomatoes. Continue these alternate layers until the dish is full. Make a boiled sauce of two tablespoonfuls of butter, one and one half-tablespoonfuls of flour, one cup of milk, and the yolks of two eggs, lastly add three tablespoonfuls of grated cheese and the beaten whites of the two eggs. Pour into the baking dish and cover all with a layer of bread crumbs dotted with bits of butter. Bake one half hour.

TO CRISP CELERY.

Let it lie in ice water two hours before serving. To fringe the stalk, stick several coarse needles into a cork and draw the stalk half way from the top several times, and lay in the refrigerator to curl and crisp.

CELERY A LA VERSAILLES.

Cleanse two or three heads of well-blanched celery and trim them nicely, leaving on just as much of the stalk as is tender; parboil the vegetable in well-salted water, then rinse in cold water and drain on a sieve. Have about a pint of boiling white stock ready in a saucepan, lay in the celery, with a large onion cut in quarters and a good seasoning of salt and pepper, and cook very gently until the celery is quite tender, then drain the vegetable carefully on a napkin so as to absorb the moisture, and cut each head into quarters lengthwise. Fold the pieces into as neat a shape as possible and make them even in size; mask them entirely over with thick bechamel sauce and allow this latter to stiffen; then dip the pieces in beaten egg, roll thickly in fine white bread crumbs, and fry in boiling fat. When sufficiently browned, drain on blotting-paper, and pile up high in the center of a hot dish covered with a napkin. Garnish with sprigs of fried parsley and serve.

CELERY-POTATO CROQUETTES.

To a pint of mashed potatoes add half a teacup of cooked celery, season with a tablespoon of butter, half a teaspoon of salt, a dash of white pepper; add the yolk of one egg. Roll in shape of a small cylinder three inches long and one and a fourth inches thick. Dip them in the beaten white of egg, roll in cracker or bread crumbs and fry.

CHICAGO RECORD.

CELERY AU GRATIN.

Wash and trim four heads of celery; set in a stewpan with a teaspoonful of vinegar, salt and cold water; boil until tender and drain dry. Make some sauce with a tablespoonful of butter, the same quantity of flour and half a pint of milk. Cook while stirring till it thickens; add the yolk of one egg and a tablespoonful of grated cheese; stir the sauce, but do not let it boil. Arrange the celery in a pie dish, sprinkle bread crumbs over and little bits of butter; cover with sauce and brown in the oven. Serve in the dish in which it is cooked.

CHICAGO RECORD.

CELERY SALAD.

Take the inner and tenderest heads of three stalks of celery, cut them into strips an inch long and about the thickness of young French beans. Rub the salad bowl lightly with shallot. Mix the yolks of two hard boiled eggs with three tablespoonfuls of salad oil, one of tarragon vinegar, a little mustard and pepper and salt to taste. Add the celery to this sauce, toss well with two silver forks, garnish with slices of hard boiled eggs. If you have any cold chicken or turkey, chop it up, and mix with some of above in equal proportions; or a few oysters will be a great addition.

STEWED CELERY.

After celery is cut up and soaked in cold water for fifteen minutes, then cooked until tender, it must be drained in the colander, thrown into cold water to blanch and become firm, and then thoroughly heated in a white sauce. If the cold bath is neglected the result will be flat and discolored instead of white and crisp.

CELERY SOUP.

The ingredients are two heads of celery, one quart of water, one quart of milk, two tablespoonfuls of flour, one teaspoonful of salt, two tablespoonfuls of butter and a dash of pepper. Wash and scrape celery and cut in half inch pieces, put in boiling water and cook until soft. Mash the celery in the water in which it is boiled and add salt and pepper. Let the milk come to a boil; cream together the butter and flour and stir the boiling milk into it slowly; then add celery and strain through a sieve mashing and pressing with the back of a spoon until all but the tough fibres of the celery are squeezed through. Return the soup to the fire and heat until it is steaming when it is ready to serve.

BOILED CELERIAC.

Pare the roots and throw them into cold water for one half hour. Cut into squares, boil in salted water until tender and serve with a butter or cream sauce.

CELERIAC SALAD.

Boil the roots in salted water, throw into cold water and peel; slice, serve on lettuce leaves and pour over a French or mayonnaise dressing. (See **Salad Dress-**

ing.)

CHERVIL SALAD.

Clean the leaves thoroughly in cold water and shake to drain. Serve with French salad dressing. The leaves are aromatic and are used for seasoning dressings, salads, sauces and soups and also for garnishes.

CREAM CHICORY.

Clean well and boil several heads of chicory, drain and cool; squeeze out the water from the chicory and mince it; melt some butter in a saucepan and cook until the moisture has evaporated; sprinkle with flour and add hot milk; boil up stirring all the time; season, and cook on back of the stove fifteen minutes; serve with croutons or bits of toast.

FRENCH RECIPE.

CHICORY SALAD.

Wash and shake well; select the white leaves and cut in one or two inch lengths. In the salad bowl mix the oil, salt and vinegar then add the chicory and mix vigorously with a wooden fork and spoon; add the vinegar sparingly—1 1/2 tablespoons of vinegar to 6 of oil. A crust of bread rubbed with garlic is usually added, but the bowl itself may be slightly rubbed with a cut clove.

FRENCH RECIPE.

CITRON PRESERVES.

Select sound fruit, pare and divide them into quarters, and cut each quarter into small pieces, take the seeds out carefully; the slices may be left plain or may be cut in fancy shapes, notching the edges nicely, weigh the citron, and to every pound of fruit allow a pound of sugar. Boil in water with a small piece of alum until clear and tender; then rinse in cold water. Boil the weighed sugar in water and skim until the syrup is clear. Add the fruit, a little ginger root or a few slices of lemon, boil five minutes and fill hot jars. Seal tightly.

CITRON PUDDING.

Cream together half a cup of butter and one cup of sugar; add the well beaten yolks of five eggs, the juice and grated peel of one lemon, and whip until very light, then add the whites beaten to a froth alternately with two full cups of flour, through which must be sifted two even teaspoonfuls of baking powder. Butter a mold lavishly, line it with strips of preserved citron, using a quarter of a pound for a pudding of this size, put in the batter, cover and set in a pan with boiling water in a good oven. Keep the pan nearly full of boiling water and bake steadily one and one half hours. Dip the mold in cold water, turn out upon a hot dish, and eat at once with any kind of sweet pudding sauce. The mold must not be filled more than two thirds full, in order to give the pudding a chance to swell.

SWEET PICKLED CITRON.

One pound of sugar and one quart of vinegar (if too strong dilute with water) to every two pounds of citron. Boil the vinegar, sugar and spices together and skim well. Then add the citron and cook until about half done. Use spices to suit taste.

CORN CHOWDER.

Chop fine one-quarter pound of salt pork, put in a kettle, and when well tried out add two white onions sliced thin. Brown lightly, then add one pint of raw diced potatoes, one can of corn, chopped fine, and sufficient boiling water to cover. When the potatoes are tender stir in two tablespoonfuls of flour, blended with one of butter, one teaspoonful of salt and saltspoonful of white pepper and one quart of boiling milk. Simmer five minutes longer, add one cupful of hard crackers, broken into bits, and serve.

MISS BEDFORD.

CHICKEN WITH CORN OYSTERS.

Clean and joint a chicken, one weighing about three pounds, as for fricassee. Wipe each piece with a damp cloth, dip in slightly beaten egg; then roll in seasoned fine bread crumbs. Arrange in a deep dish, and bake in a very hot oven for forty-five minutes, basting every ten minutes with melted butter. While the chicken is baking chop one cup full of cold boiled corn fine, add to it one beaten egg, one-quarter of a teaspoonful of salt, a dash of pepper, one tablespoonful of milk, two tablespoonfuls of flour and one-quarter of a teaspoonful of baking powder. Heat one tablespoonful of drippings in a pan, drop the batter in in spoonfuls, and brown quickly on both sides. Prepare a sauce with one tablespoonful of butter, blended with one of flour and one cupful of chicken stock (made from the neck and wing tips), one-half of a cupful of cream, one teaspoonful of lemon juice, a saltspoon of salt, one-quarter as much pepper and the yolks of two eggs. Do not add the eggs and cream until just before it is taken from the fire. Arrange on a warm, deep platter. Garnish with the corn oysters and sprigs of parsley. Serve the sauce in a boat.

CHICAGO RECORD.

CREAM OF CORN.

Use one can of corn for one quart of soup. Crush it thoroughly with pestle or potato-masher to free the pulp from the tough outside coating; rub through a fine colander, then through a sieve. Add one teacupful of cream to the strained pulp and enough milk to make a quart altogether. Put in a dash of cayenne pepper, a piece of butter the size of a filbert, and salt to taste—it requires a surprising amount of salt to bring out the flavor. Use a double boiler as it burns easily. Serve very hot stirring well before taking up.

MRS. THOMPSON.

GREEN CORN FRITTERS.

Cut the corn from three good sized ears and chop it slightly. Add one well beaten egg, one-half cup of milk, one tablespoonful of sugar, one-half teaspoonful of salt, one-quarter teaspoonful of pepper, and flour enough to make a thin batter. Put one teaspoonful of baking powder in the flour, fry to a golden brown in boiling fat.

CORN OMELET.

Take cold boiled corn and after cutting the grains through the middle, scrape it from the cob. Make a plain omelet, and have the corn with very little milk heating in a saucepan, seasoning to taste. When the omelet is ready to turn, put the corn by spoonfuls over half the top, and fold the omelet over. Serve at once.

GREEN CORN PUDDING.

Take one dozen ears of tender corn; grate them; then add one quart of sweet milk thickened with three tablespoonfuls of flour made free from lumps, a full tablespoonful of butter, four eggs, and pepper and salt to taste. Butter an earthen baking dish and pour into it this mixture. Bake one and one-half hours. This is to be served as a vegetable, though with the addition of sugar and a rich sauce it can be used as a dessert.

CORN SOUP.

Take three ears of corn, remove the corn from the cob and boil the cobs in three pints of soup stock or water very slowly one half hour. Remove the cobs, put in the corn and boil twenty minutes, then rub the corn through a sieve and add salt and pepper to taste. Boil up again and stir into the soup a tablespoonful of flour and butter mixed. When it thickens add one cupful of boiling milk. Let this new mixture come to a boil, add one well beaten egg and serve.

CORN VINEGAR.

Add to one gallon of rain water one pint of brown sugar or molasses and one pint of corn off the cob. Put into a jar, cover with a cloth, set in the sun, and in three weeks you will have good vinegar. Most people prefer it to cider vinegar.

CORN SALAD.

Corn salad makes a most refreshing salad in winter and spring as a substitute for lettuce. Serve with French dressing. It is also used as greens and is cooked like spinach.

CRESS.

Water cress has a pleasant and highly pungent flavor that makes it valuable as a salad or garniture. Tear water cress apart with the fingers and put them loosely in a bowl to clean; use cold water; break off the roots, do not use a knife; dress with salt, vinegar, and a little powdered sugar. Some send them to the table without any dressing and eat them with a little salt.

CUCUMBER AND CRESS SALAD.

Pare two cucumbers and cut them into quarters, lengthwise, then into half-inch pieces. Pick over, wash and drain a pint of fresh cress, and dry in a cloth. Add the cucumbers; mix and turn into the salad-bowl and pour over a French dressing, made by mixing together four tablespoonfuls of olive oil, one-quarter of a teaspoonful of salt, and the same of white pepper, then dropping in, while stirring quickly, one tablespoonful of tarragon or plain vinegar, or lemon juice.

CHICAGO RECORD.

WATER CRESS SOUP.

Look over carefully one large bunch of water cress and chop it fine. Melt one large tablespoonful of butter in a granite stew-pan, add the cress and one teaspoonful of lemon juice. Cook about ten minutes, until the cress is tender. Do not let it burn. Add one egg, well beaten, with one heaping teaspoonful of flour, also one saltspoonful of salt and two dashes of pepper. Then pour in three pints of well-flavored soup stock. Let boil five minutes longer and serve with croutons.

CHICAGO RECORD.

WATERCRESS AND WALNUT SALAD.

Crack fifty walnuts and remove the meats as nearly as possible in unbroken halves. Squeeze over them the juice of two large lemons, or three small ones, and leave them for several hours, or a day if convenient. Just before dinner pick over in a cool place one quart of watercress, wash it carefully and drain on a napkin. At the last moment drench the cress with French dressing, spread the nuts over it, give them a generous sprinkling of the dressing and serve.

Chicago Record.

BOILED CUCUMBERS.

Peel the cucumbers unless very young and tender, put into boiling salted water, and when boiled throw them into cold water to firm them. When ready for use, heat them in butter quickly without frying them, season with salt and pepper, pour over any good sauce and serve. Ripe cucumbers can be treated quite similarly unless the seeds are tough, if they are, mash the cucumbers through a sieve and serve with butter, pepper and salt.

CUCUMBER CATSUP.

Take twelve large, full-grown cucumbers and four onions. Peel the cucumbers and take the skin off the onions; grate them, and let the pulp drain through a sieve for several hours, then season highly with salt and pepper, and add good cider vinegar until the pickle tastes strongly of it, and it rises a little to the top. Put it in jars or wide-mouthed bottles, and cork or seal them so as to be airtight. The pickle tastes more like the fresh cucumber than anything else, and will pay for the making.

FRIED CUCUMBER.

Boil a good-sized cucumber till nearly soft in milk and water flavored slightly with onion. Remove and drain dry, cut it up into slices when cold and brush each slice, which should be about a third of an inch thick, with egg, and dip in bread crumbs or make a batter and dip each slice in this, after which fry in butter till amber brown. To be served in the center of a hot dish with mashed potatoes round.

CUCUMBER MANGOES.

See Mangoes.

CUCUMBER A LA POULETTE.

Pare and cut in slices three good-sized cucumbers; cover with water and let soak for half an hour, then drain and dry on a cloth. Put in a saucepan with two tablespoonfuls of butter and fry over a moderate fire without browning for five minutes. Add one scant tablespoonful of flour, and, when well mixed, one and one-half cupfuls of chicken or veal broth. Simmer gently for twenty minutes, season with a small teaspoonful of salt, a saltspoonful of pepper and half a teaspoonful of sugar; draw the pan to one side, add the beaten yolks of two eggs and one tablespoonful of finely chopped parsley. Take from the fire as soon as thickened, being careful not to allow the sauce to boil again.

Marion C. Wilson.

CUCUMBER SALAD.

Peel the cucumbers, slice as thin as possible, cover with salt, let stand one hour covered, then put in colander and let cold water run over them until all the salt is off. Make a bed of cress or lettuce leaves and pour over French dressing; or prepare as above, pour over vinegar, give a little dash of cayenne pepper and add sour cream. Cucumbers sliced very thin with a mayonnaise dressing make a very excellent sandwich filling.

CUCUMBER SALAD CUPS.

Choose medium sized cucumbers, pare carefully and cut off the two ends, cut them in halves lengthwise, take out the seeds and put the cucumbers into ice water for two hours. When ready for use wipe the cucumbers dry, set them on a bed of lettuce leaves, asparagus leaves, cress, parsley or any other pretty garniture, and fill the shells with lobster, salmon or shrimp salad, asparagus, potato or vegetable salad, mix with mayonnaise before stuffing and put a little more on top afterwards.

STUFFED CUCUMBERS.

Choose medium sized cucumbers, pare, cut off one or both ends, extract the seeds, boil from three to five minutes, drain and throw into cold water to firm, drain again and fill the insides with chicken or veal forcemeat; line a pan with thin slices of pork, on which set the cucumbers, season with salt and pepper and a pinch of marjoram and summer savory, baste with melted butter, or gravy, chicken gravy is the best, cover with a buttered paper and let bake. Or stuff with a sausage forcemeat, make a bed for the cucumbers of chopped vegetables and moisten with stock or water; or fill with a tomato stuffing as for stuffed tomatoes, baste often with butter, or a nice gravy, put over a buttered paper and bake until done, in about fifteen or twenty minutes. The Chicago Record gave the following recipe for cucumbers stuffed with rice:—Pare thinly five five-inch cucumbers. Cut off one end and remove the pulp, leaving a thick solid case, with one thick end. Season one cup of hot boiled rice, salted in cooking, with a tablespoonful of butter, a "pinch" each of marjoram and summer savory, saltspoonful of grated nutmeg, four shakes of cayenne and a tablespoonful of lemon juice. Fill the cucumbers with this mixture; replace the end, fastening it with small skewers; place in a pan of boiling water, salted, in which are two bay leaves and a clove of garlic, and boil for ten minutes or until tender. Drain and serve covered with a cream sauce.

DANDELIONS.

Use the dandelions in the early spring when they are young and tender. They take the place of spinach and are treated the same. (See **Spinach**.) Dandelions may be used as a salad with a French dressing.

EGG PLANT CROQUETTES.

Peel, slice and boil until tender, mash and season with pepper and salt; roll crackers or dry bread, and stir into it until very thick. Make into croquettes or patties; fry in hot lard or with a piece of salt pork.

ESCALLOPED EGG PLANT.

1 egg plant, 2 tablespoonfuls butter, one teaspoonful salt, 1/3 teaspoonful pepper, 1 egg, 4 tablespoonfuls grated cheese, 1 tablespoonful Worcestershire sauce, 3 tablespoonfuls bread crumbs.

One good sized perfect egg plant. Let stand in cold water one hour. Do not remove skin, but put the egg plant whole in a deep kettle of boiling water, cover, and cook thirty minutes, or until tender. Be careful not to break the skin while cooking. Drain on large platter and cool. Cut in half and turn cut surfaces to platter while removing skin with knife and fork. Egg plant discolors readily, also stains easily; so, keep covered from the air when not preparing it. Use silver knife and fork for chopping; porcelain frying pan for seasoning process and an earthen dish for baking if you desire best results. Chop the plant moderately fine, season with salt and pepper and simmer in two tablespoonfuls of butter over a slow fire for ten minutes, keeping it closely covered. Add one tablespoonful of Worcestershire Sauce after taking from the fire, and divide the mixture into two equal portions. Put the first half into a hot buttered baking dish; sprinkle over it one half of the grated cheese and one tablespoonful of bread crumbs. Stir one well beaten egg into the second portion; add to the first, cover with remainder of cheese and finish with two tablespoonfuls of bread crumbs. Bake in moderately hot oven for twenty minutes. Cover the dish for first five minutes, or until the bread crumbs shall have lightly browned. Serve hot as an entree, with or without tomato sauce, according to taste.

ALICE CAREY WATERMAN.

FRIED EGG PLANT.

Select a plant not too large or old. Cut in slices one fourth of an inch thick, and lay in weak salt water over night. In the morning remove the purple rind and wipe dry, dip in beaten egg, then in fine bread crumbs or cracker dust; fry on the griddle or in a spider in hot butter and drippings until a nice brown. It must cook rather slowly until thoroughly soft, otherwise it is unpalatable.

MRS. MALLORY.

They can be more daintily fried if they are steamed first, in which case the slices should be cut one inch thick and should lie in salt and water two hours before frying. Crumbs sifted through a coarse sieve are an improvement.

STUFFED EGG PLANT

Choose four rather small egg plants and cut in halves; with a spoon scoop out a part of the flesh from each half, leaving a thin layer adhering to the skin. Salt the shells and drain; chop the flesh. Mince two or three onions, brown with a little butter, mix with the flesh of the egg plant, and cook away the moisture; add some chopped mushrooms, parsley and lastly an equal quantity of bread crumbs. Season with salt and pepper, remove from the fire and thicken with yolks of eggs. Now fill the shells, dust with bread crumbs, put in a baking-pan and sprinkle with olive oil, or bits of butter and bake.

FRENCH RECIPE.

ENDIVE SALAD.

Endive is wholesome and delicate. If the curled endive be prepared, use only the yellow leaves, removing the thick stalks and cutting the small ones into thin pieces; the smooth endive stalk as well must be cut fine. It may be mixed with oil, vinegar, salt and pepper, and a potato mashed fine, or with sour cream mixed with oil, vinegar and salt. When mixed with the last dressing it is usually served with hot potatoes. Endive may also be used as spinach. (See **Spinach** Recipes.)

A FLOWER SALAD.

The most beautiful salad ever imagined is rarely seen upon our tables, although the principal material for its concoction may be grown in the tiniest yard. Any one who has tried growing nasturtiums must admit that they almost take care of themselves, and if the ground is enriched but a little their growth and yield of blossom is astonishingly abundant. It is these same beautiful blossoms that are used in salad, and, as if nature had surmised that their beauty should serve the very practical end of supplying the salad bowl, the more one plucks these growing flowers, the greater number will a small plant yield. The pleasant, pungent flavor of these blossoms would recommend them, aside from their beauty, and when they are shaken out of ice-cold water with some bits of heart lettuce, they, too, become crisp in their way. One of the prettiest ways of arranging a nasturtium salad is to partly fill the bowl with the center of a head of lettuce pulled apart and the blossoms plentifully scattered throughout. Prof. Blot, that prince of saladmakers, recommends the use of the blossoms and petals (not the leaves) of roses, pinks, sage, lady's slipper, marshmallow and periwinkle, as well as the nasturtium, for decorating the ordinary lettuce salad, and reminds his readers that roses and pinks may be had at all seasons of the year. In summer the lovely pink marshmallow is to be found wild in the country places near salt water; so abundant are these flowers in the marshes (hence the name) and so large are the petals that there need be no fear of robbing the flower vases to fill the salad bowl. These salads should be dressed at the table by the mistress, as, of course, a little wilting is sure to follow if the seasoning has been applied for any length of time. A French dressing is the best, although a mayonnaise may be used if preferred. Opinions differ greatly as regards the proportions of the former, but to quote Blot again, the proper ones are two of oil to one of vinegar, pepper and salt to taste. If the eye is not trained to measure pepper and salt and the hostess is timid about dressing a salad, let her have measured in a pretty cut-glass sprinkler a teaspoon of salt and half of pepper mixed, for every two of oil. For a small salad the two of oil and one of vinegar will be sufficient; measure the saltspoon even full of oil, sprinkle this over the salad, then half the salt and pepper; toss all lightly with the spoon and fork, then add the other spoonful of oil, the vinegar and the remainder of the salt and pepper; toss well and serve. How simple, and yet there are women who never have done the graceful thing of dressing lettuce at the table.

Rebecca Underwood.

Potatoes and tomatoes in alternate layers may take the place of lettuce. Just before serving toss all together.

FLOWER SANDWICHES.

Make a filling of two-thirds nasturtium blossoms, one third leaves, lay on buttered bread, with buttered bread on top, sandwich style.

Chicago Record.

PRESERVED ROSE LEAVES.

Put a layer of rose leaves in a jar and sprinkle sugar over them, add layers sprinkled with sugar as the leaves are gathered until the jar is full. They will turn dark brown and will keep for two or three years. Used in small quantities they add a delightful flavor to fruit cake and mince pies.

Mrs. Rollins.

SACHET POWDERS.

In making sachet powders one general direction must be borne in mind—each ingredient must be powdered before mixing. Potpourri should be made before the season of outdoor flowers passes. Pluck the most fragrant flowers in your garden, passing by all withered blossoms. Pick the flowers apart, placing the petals on plates and setting them where the sun can shine upon them. Let the petals thus continue to dry in the sun for several days. Each flower may be made into potpourri by itself, or the different flowers may be mixed in any variety and proportion that pleases the maker. Flowers which have little or no scent should be left out. When the leaves are well dried sprinkle them with table salt. Do not omit this, as it is important. The right proportion is about two ounces of the salt to each pound of leaves. If also two ounces of powdered orris root is added and well mixed in with the dried petals the fragrance and permanence are improved. Now the potpourri is ready to put in the jars that are sold for that purpose.

H. J. Hancock.

VIOLET MARMALADE.

Crush three pounds of violets to a pulp; in the meantime boil four pounds of sugar, take out some, blow through it, and if little flakes of sugar fly from it, it is done. Add the flowers, stir them together; add two pounds of apple marmalade, and when it has boiled up a few times, put the marmalade into jars.

The Cook's Own Book.

GARLIC BUTTER SAUCE.

Bruise half a dozen cloves of garlic, rub them through a fine sieve with a wooden spoon; mix this pulp with butter and beat thoroughly, put in a wide mouthed bottle and keep for further use.

GROUND CHERRY PUDDING.

Half fill a pudding dish with ripe ground cherries or husk tomatoes, dot with bits of butter and cover with a soft batter made of one cup milk, one egg, one tablespoonful butter, two teaspoonfuls baking powder and a half-saltspoonful of salt. Bake quickly and serve with lemon sauce. This fruit is so easily raised, so prolific and so delicious, used in various ways, that I wonder it is not more widely known and used. For pies, preserves, puddings and dried, to put in cake, it is inferior to none. It will keep a long time in the husks in a dry place. It will flourish in the fence corners or any out-of-the-way place, and seems to prefer a poor soil and neglect.

Harriet I. Mann.

HERBS.

Whether food is palatable or not largely depends upon its seasoning. Good, rich material may be stale and unprofitable because of its lack, while with it simple, inexpensive foods become delicious and take on the appearance of luxuries. A garden of herbs with its varying flavors is a full storehouse for the housekeeper, it gives great variety to a few materials and without much expense of money, time or space as any little waste corner of the garden or even a window box, will afford a fine supply. Besides use as flowers the young sprouts of most of the herbs are available as greens or salads, and are excellent with any plain salad dressing; among them might be mentioned mustard, cress, chervil, parsley, mint, purslane, chives, sorrel, dandelions, nasturtiums, tarragon and fennel. Many of these herbs are ornamental and make beautiful garnishes, or are medicinal and add to the home pharmacy. Though not equally good as the fresh herbs, yet dried ones hold their flavors and do excellent service. Just before flowering they should be gathered on a sunshiny day and dried by artificial heat, as less flavor escapes in quick drying. When dry, powder them and put up in tin cans, or glass bottles, tightly sealed and properly labeled. Parsley, mint and tarragon should be dried in June or July, thyme, marjoram and savory in July and August, basil and sage in August and September.

Anise.—Anise leaves are used for garnishing, and the seeds for seasoning, also are used medicinally.

Balm.—Balm leaves and stems are used medicinally and make a beverage called Balm Wine. A variety of cat-mint called Moldavian balm is used in Germany for flavoring food.

Basil.—Sweet basil an aromatic herb is classed among the sweet herbs. It is used as seasoning in soups, sauces, salads and in fish dressings. Basil vinegar takes the place in winter of the fresh herb.

Basil Vinegar.—In August or September gather the fresh basil leaves. Clean them thoroughly, put them in a wide mouthed bottle and cover with cider vinegar, or wine for fourteen days. If extra strength is wanted draw off the vinegar after a week or ten days and pour over fresh leaves; strain after fourteen days and bottle tightly.

Borage.—Its pretty blue flowers are used for garnishing salads. The young leaves and tender tops are pickled in vinegar and are occasionally boiled for the table. Its leaves are mucilaginous and are said to impart a coolness to beverages in which they are steeped. Borage, wine, water, lemon and sugar make an English drink called Cool Tankard.

Caraway.—Caraway seeds are used in cakes, breads, meats, pastry and candies and are very nice on mutton or lamb when roasting. Caraway and dill are a great addition to bean soup. The root though strong flavored is sometimes used like parsnips and carrots.

Catnip or Catmint.—Its leaves are used medicinally and its young leaves and shoots are used for seasoning.

Chives.—The young leaves of chives are used for seasoning, they are like the onion but more delicate, and are used to flavor sauces, salads, dressings and soups. They are chopped very fine when added to salads—sometimes the salad bowl is only rubbed with them. Chopped very fine and sprinkled over Dutch cheese they make a very acceptable side dish or sandwich filling.

Coriander.—Coriander seed is used in breads, cakes and candies.

Dill.—The leaves are used in pickles, sauces and gravies, and the seeds, in soups, curries and medicines.

Fennel.—The leaves of the common fennel have somewhat the taste of cucumber, though they are sweet and have a more delicate odor. They are boiled and served chiefly with mackerel and salmon though sometimes with other fish, or enter into the compound of their sauces. The young sprouts from the roots of sweet fennel when blanched are a very agreeable salad and condiment. The seed is medicinal.

Henbane.—Henbane is poisonous and is only used medicinally.

Hops.—The young shoots of hops are used as vegetables in the early spring, prepared in the same way as asparagus and salsify. The leaves are narcotic and are therefore often made up into pillows.

Horehound.—The leaves are used for seasoning and are a popular remedy for a cough. It is much used in flavoring candies.

Hyssop.—The young leaves and shoots are used for flavoring food, but their principal use is medicinal. A syrup made from it is a popular remedy for a cold.

Lavender.—The leaves are used for seasoning, but the chief use of the plant is the distillation of perfumery from its flowers which are full of a sweet odor.

Marjoram Sweet.—Sweet marjoram belongs to the sweet herbs, the leaves and ends of the shoots are used for seasoning, and are also used medicinally.

Pennyroyal.—The leaves are used for seasoning puddings and other dishes, and also have a medicinal use.

Pot Marigold.—Marigold has a bitter taste, but was formerly much used in seasoning soups and is still in some parts of England. The flowers are dried and are used medicinally and for coloring butter and cheese.

Pimpinella, or Salad-Burnet.—The young tender leaves are used as a salad; they have a flavor resembling that of cucumbers.

Rosemary.—A distillation of the leaves makes a pleasant perfume and is also used medicinally. It is one of the sweet herbs for seasoning.

Rue.—This is one of the bitter herbs yet is sometimes used for seasoning.

Saffron.—The dried pistils are used for flavoring and dyeing. Some people use it with rice. It is often used in fancy cooking as a coloring material.

Sage.—The leaves both fresh and dried are used for seasoning, meats and dressings especially.

Summer Savory.—Summer savory is used for flavoring, and especially for flavoring beans.

Tarragon or Esdragon.—Esdragon with its fine aromatic flavor is a valuable adjunct to salads and sauces.

Tarragon or Esdragon Vinegar.—Strip the leaves from the fresh cut stalks of tarragon. Put a cupful of them in a wide mouthed bottle and cover with a quart of cider or wine vinegar, after fourteen days, strain, bottle and cork tightly.

Tagetis Lucida.—Its leaves have almost the exact flavor of tarragon and can be used as its substitute.

Thyme.—Thyme is one of the sweet herbs and its leaves are favorites for seasoning in cooking.

Winter Savory.—The leaves and young shoots, like summer savory are used for flavoring foods.

Wormwood.—Wormwood is used medicinally as its name implies.

HORSERADISH CREAM APPLE SAUCE.

Stew six sour apples and sift; let cool, and add two heaping tablespoonfuls of grated horseradish; when cold and ready to serve add double the amount of whipped cream, slightly sweetened.

CHICAGO RECORD.

KALE.

See Borecole.

KOHL RABI.

Strip the leaves from the stem, put on in salted water and boil. Peel the tubers, slice thin and boil until tender; drain and chop very fine both leaves and tubers separately, then mix thoroughly; brown a tablespoonful of butter and a little flour in a saucepan, add the kohl rabi and cook for a moment, then add a cup of meat broth and boil thoroughly; serve very hot.

LEAVES FOR CULINARY PURPOSES.

In addition to sweet and bitter herbs, we have many leaves available for seasoning. The best known and most used are bay leaves, a leaf or two in custards, rice, puddings and soups adds a delicate flavor and aroma. A laurel leaf answers the same purpose. Bitter almond flavoring has a substitute in fresh peach leaves which have a smell and taste of bitter almond. Brew the leaves, fresh or dry, and use a teaspoonful or two of the liquid. Use all these leaves stintedly as they are strongly aromatic, and it is easy to get too much. The flowering currant gives a flavor that is a compound of the red and black currant; gooseberry leaves in the bottled fruit emphasize the flavor, and it is said keep the fruit greener. A fresh geranium or lemon verbena leaf gives a delightful odor and taste to jelly. A geranium leaf or two in the bottom of a cake dish while the cake is baking will flavor the cake. Nasturtium leaves and flowers find a place in sandwiches and salads. The common syringa has an exact cucumber flavor and can be a substitute for cucumber in salads or wherever that flavor is desired. Lemon and orange leaves answer for the juice of their fruits. Horseradish and grape leaves have use in pickles. Carrot, cucumber and celery leaves give the respective flavors of their vegetables. Tender celery leaves can be thoroughly dried and bottled for winter use. The use of leaves is an economy for a household, and a source of great variety.

LEEKS.

Leeks are generally used to flavor soups, sauces and salads and are seldom brought to the table as a separate dish. However, they are semi-occasionally served as follows:—Boiled and dressed with a cream sauce; or when two-thirds done are put to soak in vinegar seasoned with salt, pepper and cloves, then are drained, stuffed, dipped in batter and fried.

BOILED LETTUCE.

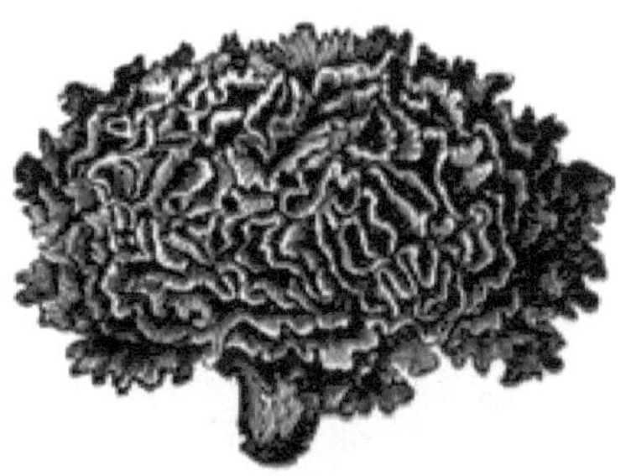

Take the coarser part of lettuce not delicate enough for a salad, boil in salted water until soft, then drain thoroughly. Slightly brown a tablespoonful of butter and a dessertspoonful of flour in a saucepan, put in the lettuce, let it cook up once or twice, then add a half-cup of stock and boil thoroughly, just before serving add a gill of cream and give a sprinkle of nutmeg if the flavor is liked.

LETTUCE SALAD.

Lettuce leaves whole or shredded are served with vinegar, salt, pepper, mustard and a little sugar, or with a French or mayonnaise dressing; or it is shredded and mixed with veal and egg, sweetbreads, shrimps, cress, cucumber, tomatoes or other salad material and is treated with the various salad dressings, mentioned above.

STEWED GREEN PEAS WITH LETTUCE.

Shell a half peck of peas, and shred two heads of lettuce; boil together with as little water as possible to keep it from burning, and stir often for the same purpose. Stew one hour, set back on the stove, and add one tablespoonful of butter, one teaspoonful of sugar, salt, and a dash of cayenne pepper and just as it is taken up, one well beaten egg, which must not be allowed to boil. Serve at once.

STUFFED LETTUCE.

Use five clean heads of lettuce, wash thoroughly, open up the leaves and fill between with any highly seasoned meat—sweetbreads, chicken or veal preferred—or make a forcemeat stuffing. Tie up the heads, put into a saucepan with any good gravy, stock or sauce and cook until thoroughly heated through; serve in the gravy.

LETTUCE SOUP.

Use three small lettuce heads, clean, drain, chop and put into a saucepan with a tablespoonful of butter, cover and let steam for a few minutes, then add two quarts of good soup stock or one quart each of stock and milk, add a half-cup of rice and boil until the rice is soft. Strain through a sieve, or not, as one fancies, season with salt, pepper, return to the fire, add a pint of cream, let it come just to the boiling point and serve.

MANGOES.

Mangoes are made from cucumbers, melons, peppers, tomatoes and peaches. The following recipe applies to all but the peaches. Select green or half grown melons and large green cucumbers, tomatoes, or peppers. Remove a narrow piece the length of the fruit, and attach it at one end by a needle and white thread, after the seeds of the mango have been carefully taken out. Throw the mangoes into a brine of salt and cold water strong enough to bear up an egg, and let them remain in it three days and nights, then throw them into fresh cold water for twenty-four hours. If grape leaves are at hand, alternate grape leaves and mangoes in a porcelain kettle (never a copper one) until all are in, with grape leaves at the bottom and top. Add a piece of alum the size of a walnut, cover with cider vinegar and boil fifteen minutes. Remove the grape leaves and stuff the mangoes. Prepare a cabbage, six tomatoes, a few small cucumbers and white onions, by chopping the cabbage and tomatoes and putting all separately into brine for twenty-four hours and draining thoroughly. After draining chop the cucumbers and onions. Drain the mangoes, put into each a teaspoonful of sugar, and two whole cloves. Add to the vegetable filling, one-fourth ounce each of ground ginger, black pepper, mace, allspice, nasturtium seed, ground cinnamon, black and white mustard, one-fourth cup of horseradish and one-fourth cup sweet oil. Bruise all the spices and mix with the oil, then mix all the ingredients thoroughly and stuff the mangoes, fit the piece taken out and sew in with white thread or tie it in with a string around the mango. Put them into a stone jar and pour over them hot cider vinegar sweetened with a pound or more of sugar to the gallon to suit the taste. If they are not keeping properly pour over again fresh hot vinegar.

MARTYNIAS.

Gather the pods when young and tender enough to thrust a needle through them easily, later they become hard and useless for pickles. Leave half an inch of stem on each, and lay them in salt water a couple of days, then cook in weak vinegar until tender, but not so long as to break them. Drain well from this, place them in jars and prepare vinegar for them in the proportion of an ounce each of cloves, allspice and black pepper to a gallon of vinegar; scald all these together with half a teaspoonful of prepared mustard. Pour hot over the martynias, cover closely and keep in a cool place. They will soon be ready for use.

Mrs. Hood.

MELON, MUSK.

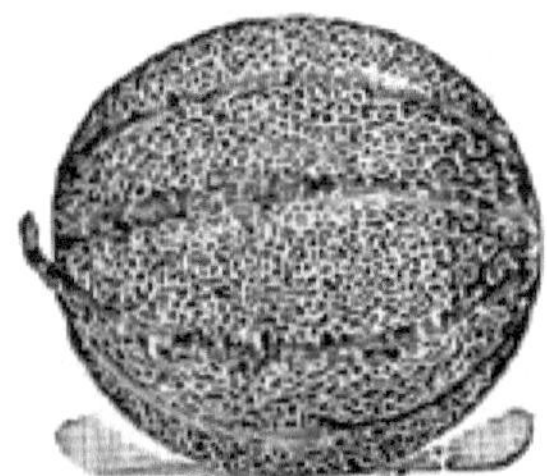

It is said a muskmelon can be chosen by its odor. If it has none, it is not good, if sweet and musky it is quite sure to be ripe. Another indication of ripeness is when the smooth skin between the rough sections is yellowish green. To serve, cut the melons crosswise and fill with chopped ice an hour before using. Try pouring a little strained honey into the melon when eating.

CANTALOUPE FRAPPE.

Select two large cantaloupes that are ripe and of fine flavor; cut into halves and scrape the pulp from same after removing the seeds (not using any of the rind); put the pulp through a potato ricer, which will keep out all the stringy parts; add to the pulp a pinch of salt, four tablespoonfuls of powdered sugar and a gill of cherry juice (sweetened with a spoonful of sugar), or use some other nice tart juice. Soak a tablespoonful of gelatine in a quarter-cupful of water; then set cup in pan of boiling water until it is dissolved; add this to the prepared cantaloupe and when cold turn into a freezer and freeze slowly. Serve in sherbet glasses.

Mrs. Sadette Harrington.

COOKED MUSKMELON.

Miss Corson, in one of her lectures, gives the following directions for making a very nice dessert from muskmelons:—Make a rich syrup from a pound of white sugar to half a pint of water. Pare and slice the melon and boil it gently in the syrup five to ten minutes flavoring with vanilla or lemon. Then take it up in the dish in which it is to be served, cool the syrup and pour it on the melon. To be eaten cold.

MELON MANGOES.

See Mangoes.

MUSKMELON PICKLE.

Use ripe muskmelons, pare, remove seeds, and cut in pieces and put into a stone jar. Cover with scalded vinegar and let them stand until the next day, when the vinegar must be reheated and poured over them again; repeat this until the fourth day, then weigh the melons and to every five pounds of the fruit allow three pounds of sugar and one quart of vinegar with spices to suit. Let all simmer together until the fruit is tender. The second day pour off this syrup, and boil down until it shall only just cover the melons. The result justifies the pains taken.

MELON, WATER.

The following is said to be an infallible sign of a ripe watermelon, it takes close inspection to find sometimes, but the sign is there if the condition for it exists. When the flesh of the melon changes color and its seeds begin to turn black a small scale or blister appears on the rind. They increase in number and size as the melon ripens, until a ripe one shows them thickly strewn over the surface. A small crop of blisters indicates unripe fruit. A melon must be served ice cold. Cut it through the middle, scoop out the flesh with a tablespoon in a circle as much as possible that the pieces may be conical or egg shaped. Cover the platter with grape leaves and pile the fruit upon them, allowing the tendrils of the grapes to wander in and out among the melon cones.

WATERMELON ICE.

Cut a watermelon in halves, scoop out the entire center, taking out the seeds; chop in tray; add a cup of sugar. Pack the freezer, turn a few minutes. It will be like soft snow and delicious.

WATERMELON PICKLES.

Eat the flesh and save the rind. Cut the rind into finger lengths and about an inch in width, pare and cut out all the red flesh, throw into a strong salt brine and let stand over night. In the morning drain, boil in water until the pickles are clear, drain again and put into a stone jar. To one gallon of fruit, allow one quart of sugar and one pint of vinegar. Do up cinnamon and cloves in little bags, in ratio of two of cinnamon to one of cloves and boil them in the syrup. Pour the boiling syrup over the pickles, tie up close and in a few days they are ready for use.

MINT SAUCE.

Four dessert spoons of chopped mint, two of sugar, one quarter pint of vinegar. Stir all together; make two or three hours before needed.

MINT VINEGAR.

Fill a bottle loosely with fresh, clean mint, pour over good vinegar, cork tightly and let stand two or three weeks. Then pour off and keep well corked. Use this vinegar as a condiment, or put a small quantity into drawn butter sauce for mutton.

MUSHROOMS.

The highest authorities say an edible mushroom can easily be distinguished from a poisonous one by certain characteristics;—a true mushroom grows only in pastures, never in wet, boggy places, never in woods, never about stumps of trees, they are of small size, dry, and if the flesh is broken it remains white or nearly so and has a pleasant odor. Most poisonous varieties change to yellow or dark brown and have a disagreeable odor, though there is a white variety which grows in woods or on the borders of woods, that is very poisonous. The cap of a true mushroom has a frill, the gills are free from the stem, they never grow down against it, but usually there is a small channel all around the top of the stem, the spores are brown-black, or deep purple black and the stem is solid or slightly pithy. It is said if salt is sprinkled on the gills and they become yellow the mushroom is poisonous, if black, they are wholesome. Sweet oil is its antidote.

BAKED MUSHROOMS.

Hold the mushrooms by the stems, dip them in boiling hot water a moment to help loosen the skin, cut off their stems. Boil the parings and stems and strain. Pour this water over the mushrooms chopped fine, add parsley and stew about forty minutes. Then add six eggs well beaten. Pour this mixture into buttered cups and bake quickly. Serve with cream sauce.

MUSHROOM CATSUP.

Boil one peck of mushrooms fifteen minutes in half a pint of water, strain, or not, through a sieve to get all the pulp; add a pint of vinegar to the juice, two tablespoonfuls of salt, one half a teaspoonful of cayenne pepper, two tablespoonfuls of mustard, one of cinnamon and one of cloves. Let the mixture boil twenty minutes; bottle and seal tightly.

FRIED MUSHROOMS.

Pare the mushrooms, cut off their stems, lay them on their heads in a frying pan in which a tablespoonful of butter has been melted, put a bit of butter into each cap, let them cook in their own liquor and the butter until thoroughly done. Season with salt and butter and serve hot.

MUSHROOMS WITH MACARONI.

Boil half a pound of macaroni. Put a pint of water, one small onion, a sprig of parsley, the juice of half a lemon, a teaspoonful of salt and a quarter as much pepper into a saucepan. When boiling add a quart of mushrooms and cook five minutes. Beat three eggs, stir in and take from the fire. Drain the macaroni, put a layer in the bottom of a baking dish, then a layer of the mushroom mixture, and thus alternately until the dish is full. Have mushrooms on top, and set in a hot oven for five minutes.

Mrs. Eliza Parker.

MARROW WITH MUSHROOMS.

Procure a shinbone and have the butcher split it; remove the marrow and cut it into inch-thick slices; then boil it one and one-half minutes in a quart of salted water, using a teaspoonful of salt. Into a frying-pan put a tablespoonful of butter; when hot add five tablespoonfuls of chopped mushrooms and toss for five minutes, sprinkling them with three shakes of salt and a speck of cayenne. Drain the marrow; squeeze over it ten drops of lemon juice; then mix with it the mushrooms; spread on slices of hot, crisp toast and serve immediately.

Chicago Record.

MUSHROOM OMELET.

Cook a dozen small, even sized mushrooms in a saucepan with half an ounce of butter and half a saltspoonful of salt sprinkled over them. Make ready a plain omelet, as it cooks at the edges place the mushrooms over one half of it, fold over the other half, slip from the pan on to a hot dish and serve immediately.

MUSHROOMS ON TOAST.

Prepare enough mushrooms to measure one half-pint when chopped, and enough of raw ham to fill a tablespoon heaping full. Mix these and add a teaspoonful of parsley, a trifle of chopped onion if liked, a teaspoonful of lemon juice, pepper and salt. Fry in two tablespoonfuls of butter, add a half-cupful of milk or cream, boil up again, and add an egg thoroughly beaten. Serve on small squares of toast. This with the addition of bread crumbs before the milk is added and with the use of some of the relishing herbs makes an excellent stuffing.

MUSHROOM SOUP.

Get your butcher to crack for you a shank of beef. Put over it four quarts of water. Let it boil hard for a few moments until all the scum has risen and has been removed. Set it back on the stove now to simmer five hours. At the end of the fourth hour add one carrot, one turnip, one small onion, one bunch of parsley, two stalks of celery, twelve cloves and two bay leaves. Let all these boil together one hour, then strain and set away until the next day, when all the grease must be skimmed off. To every quart of the stock add a quart of milk thickened with two tablespoonfuls of flour and two tablespoonfuls of butter, one saltspoonful of salt and a dust of pepper, add to this a half-pint of canned mushrooms or small mushrooms stewed thoroughly in the liquor obtained from boiling and straining the stems and parings.

MUSTARD.

In early spring the young leaves are used as a garnish, or, finely cut, as a seasoning to salads. The Cabbage Leaved Mustard makes an excellent green, and is treated like spinach.

AROMATIC MUSTARD.

Upon one tablespoonful of grated horseradish, an ounce of bruised ginger root, and five long red peppers pour half a pint of boiling vinegar. Allow to stand, closely covered, for two days; then take five teaspoonfuls of ground mustard, one teaspoonful of curry powder, and a dessertspoonful of salt, and mix well together. Strain the vinegar upon this, adding a dash of cayenne if wanted very pungent. Mix very smoothly and keep in a corked bottle or jar.

NASTURTIUM.

The flowers are used to garnish salads, the young leaves and flowers make a lovely salad (See **Flower Salad**). The young buds and leaves when tender are made into pickles and are used like capers in sauces, salads and pickles.

NASTURTIUM PICKLES.

Gather the seeds as soon as the blossoms fall, throw them into cold salt water for two days, at the end of that time cover them with cold vinegar, and when all the seed is gathered and so prepared, turn over them fresh boiling hot vinegar plain or spiced with cloves, cinnamon, mace, pepper, broken nutmeg, bay leaves and horseradish. Cork tightly.

BOILED OKRA OR GUMBO.

The long seed pod is the edible part of this plant, it can be canned or dried for winter use. If dried let it soak an hour or so before using. To cook, cut the pods in rings, boil them in salted water until tender which will be in about twenty minutes. Add butter, salt, pepper and cream. Thin muslin bags are sometimes made to hold the whole pods without breaking. After boiling tender, pour them out, season with butter, salt and pepper and bake for five minutes.

FRIED OKRA.

Cut it lengthwise, salt and pepper it, roll it in flour and fry in butter, lard or drippings.

OKRA FRITTERS.

Boil the okra, cut in slices, make a batter as for batter cakes, dip the okra in and fry in plenty of hot lard.

Mrs. E. C. Dubb.

OKRA GUMBO SOUP.

Use two quarts of tomatoes to one quart of okra cut in rings; put them over the fire with about three quarts of water and let the mixture come to a boil; take one chicken; cut it up and fry brown with plenty of gravy; put it in with the okra and tomatoes; add several small onions chopped fine, a little corn and lima beans, if they are at hand, and salt and pepper. Let all simmer gently for several hours. To be served with a tablespoonful of rice and a green garden pepper cut fine to each soup plate.

ONIONS.

Peel and slice onions under water to keep the volatile oil from the eyes. A cup of vinegar boiling on the stove modifies the disagreeable odor of onions cooking. Boil a frying pan in water with wood ashes, potash, or soda in it to remove the odor and taste of onions. To rub silver with lemon removes the onion taste from it. Leaves of parsley eaten like cress with vinegar hide the odor of onions in the breath. Onions to be eaten raw or cooked will lose their rank flavor if they are pulled and thrown into salt water an hour before use. Two waters in boiling accomplish the same purpose.

ONION FLAVORING.

To prepare onion flavoring for a vegetable soup, peel a large onion, stick several cloves into it and bake until it is brown. This gives a peculiar and excellent flavor.

FRIED APPLES AND ONIONS.

Take one part onion to two parts apple. Slice the apples without paring, and slice the onions very thin. Fry together in butter, keeping the frying pan covered, to hold the steam which prevents burning. A very slight sprinkling of sugar seems to give an added flavor. Add just as it is to be taken up or else it will burn.

ONION OMELET.

Put a lump of butter or dripping in a frying pan, then put in sliced onions, salt and pepper, cook slowly until done, but not brown. Beat the eggs, allowing two for each person, pour in the frying pan, add a little salt and stir until set. Serve hot.

ONION PICKLES.

Choose small uniform onions; make a brine that will hold up an egg, and pour over the onions boiling hot. Let them lie in this twenty-four hours, then drain and wipe dry and put into bottles. Pour over them cold cider vinegar, seasoned with sliced horseradish, whole pepper and mace. Put in bottles and seal.

BAKED ONIONS.

Boil in milk and water until just done, then drain and put them in a buttered frying pan. Put a bit of butter, salt, and pepper on each one, and add a little of the water in which the onions have boiled. Brown them quickly and serve at once.

CREAM ONIONS.

Boil onions in two waters and drain; pour over them a little boiling milk and set over the fire, add butter, cream, salt and pepper and serve hot.

ESCALLOPED ONIONS.

Boil onions in salted water with a little milk until they are tender. Put a layer of onions in a baking dish, scatter bread crumbs over them, dot with butter, season with pepper and salt and a dash of powdered sage, repeat this until the dish is full, pour over a half-cup of cream or milk. Cover the top with bread crumbs dotted with butter. Bake a light brown and serve.

STUFFED ONIONS.

Boil onions one hour in slightly salted water, and remove the centers. Make a stuffing of minced liver or chicken in these proportions; to one pound of meat one third of a cupful of gravy milk or cream, one half-cupful of fine bread crumbs, one egg, pepper and salt and some of the onion taken from the centers, mix well and fill the onion shells, dust over a few bread crumbs, dot with butter and bake until brown. Put the remaining onion into a stew pan, with a tablespoonful of butter, a half-tablespoonful of flour, and after it boils up once, add a half-cup of milk, a teaspoonful of parsley, salt and pepper, boil up again, pour over onions and serve. This is a good second course after soup served with apple sauce.

PARSLEY.

Parsley is the prime favorite of the garnishes. Its pretty curled leaves are used to decorate fish flesh and fowl and many a vegetable. Either natural, minced or fried, it is an appetizing addition to many sauces, soups, dressings and salads.

FRIED PARSLEY.

Wash the parsley very clean, chop fine and fry in butter in the proportion of one tablespoonful of butter to one pint of minced parsley. When soft, sprinkle with bread crumbs, moisten with a little water, and cook ten or fifteen minutes longer. Garnish it with sliced boiled egg. To be eaten with pigeon.

PARSLEY VINEGAR.

Fill a preserving bottle with parsley leaves, freshly gathered and washed, and cover with vinegar. Screw down the top and set aside for two or three weeks. Then strain off the vinegar, add salt and cayenne pepper to taste, bottle and cork. Use on cold meats, cabbage, etc.

PARSLEY SAUCE.

See Sauces.

BOILED PARSNIPS.

Wash, scrape and cut them into slices about an inch thick, put them in a saucepan with salted water and cook until tender, drain, cover with good rich milk, season with butter, pepper and salt to taste, bring to a boil and serve.

BROILED PARSNIPS.

After parsnips are boiled, slice and broil brown. Make a gravy as for beefsteak.

BROWNED PARSNIPS.

Put two or three thin slices of salt pork in the bottom of a kettle and let them brown, scrape and slice the parsnips and pare about the same amount of potatoes, leaving them whole if they are small. Place in alternate layers in the kettle, and add sufficient water to cook them, leaving them to brown slightly. They must be closely watched as they burn very easily. Requires about one and a half hours to cook and brown nicely. Remove the vegetables and thicken the gravy with a little flour; add pepper and salt, and a small lump of butter. Serve pork and vegetables on a large, deep platter and pour over the gravy.

FRIED PARSNIPS.

Scrape and wash parsnips, cut off the small end and cut the thick part into half-inch-thick slices. Put them in boiling water with a tablespoonful each of salt and sugar. Boil an hour or until nearly done and drain; beat two eggs, four table-spoonfuls of flour and half a pint of milk together, season with salt and pepper. Dip the slices of parsnip into the batter, then in bread crumbs and fry in boiling lard or drippings until a golden brown. Pile them in a heap on a napkin and serve very hot.

PARSNIP FRITTERS.

Scrape and halve the parsnips, boil tender in salted water, mash smooth, picking out the woody bits; then add a beaten egg to every four parsnips, a tablespoon-ful of flour, pepper and salt to taste, and enough milk to make into a thin batter; drop by the tablespoonful into hot lard, and fry brown. Drain into a hot colander and dish.

MASHED PARSNIPS.

Boil parsnips tender in salted water, drain and mash them through a colander. Put the pulp into a saucepan with two or three tablespoonfuls of cream and a small lump of butter rubbed in flour, stir them over the fire until the butter is melted and serve.

MOCK OYSTERS.

Use three grated parsnips, three eggs, one teaspoonful of salt, one teacupful of sweet cream, butter half the size of an egg, three tablespoonfuls of flour. Fry as pancakes.

PARSNIP PUFFS.

Take one egg, well beaten, and add (without stirring until the ingredients are in) one teacupful each of cold water and flour, one heaping teaspoonful of baking powder, half a teaspoonful of salt, one teacupful of well-mashed, boiled parsnips;

stir very lightly and only enough to mix. Do not let it stand long. Drop by the tablespoonful into hot, melted fat in a frying pan, and cook until a delicate brown.

CHICAGO RECORD.

AMBUSHED PEAS.

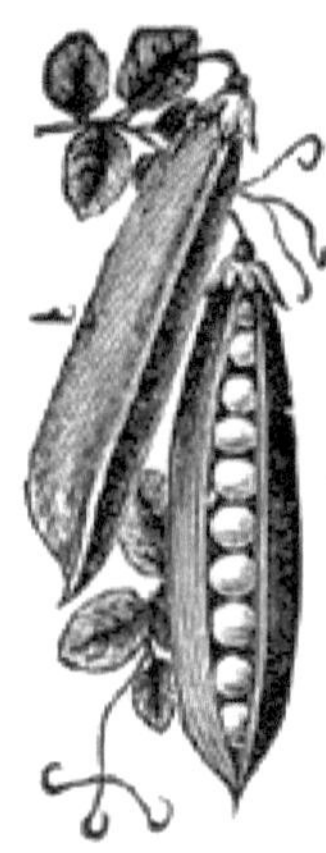

Cut the tops off of biscuits or buns twenty-four hours old. Scoop out the inside and put both shells and tops into the oven to crust. Pour into them peas after they have been boiled and mixed with a cream sauce to which an egg has been added, also minced parsley or mint if liked. Cover carefully with the tops and serve hot.

BOILED PEAS.

Do not shell peas until ready to cook. Salt, and slightly sweeten if needed boiling water, drop the peas so slowly into the water it will not stop boiling. Boil the peas until tender without covering and they will keep their color. They will generally cook in about twenty minutes, take them up with a little of the liquor in which they were boiled, butter and pepper them, and they are much better to add a little sweet cream, but will do without. If they are cooked immediately upon gathering, they will need no sugar; if allowed to remain twelve hours or more, a tablespoonful of sugar will be found an addition. A sprig of mint or a little parsley may be added. Pea-pods are sometimes boiled in a small quantity of water, then are skimmed out and the peas are boiled in this liquor.

PEAS AND BUTTERED EGGS.

Stew a pint of young peas with a tablespoonful of butter, a little salt, pepper and chopped parsley, until they are tender; beat up two eggs and pour over them the boiling peas. Serve at once on toast before the eggs harden.

CANAPES OF PEAS.

These form a dainty entree. To prepare the canapes take some slices of stale bread about two inches thick and cut into neat rounds with a large biscuit cutter. With a smaller cutter mark a circle in the center of each round and scoop out the crumbs from it to the depth of one inch. This must be carefully done, so there will be a firm bottom and sides. Lay these around in a shallow dish and pour over them a half-pint of milk in which one egg has been thoroughly beaten. This proportion of egg and milk is sufficient for six canapes. Let them lie in this for a few minutes; then take up very carefully and slip into very hot lard. When of a pale golden brown remove with a skimmer and drain on blotting paper. Boil a pint of freshly cleaned peas in unsalted water until tender; drain well. Put into a saucepan with two spoons of butter, dredge in a dessertspoonful of flour and add a saltspoon of salt and a quarter of a pint of milk. Let it come to a boil; then fill the canapes with this, give a dusting of pepper on the top of each, arrange on a platter and garnish with parsley and slices of lemon.

CHICAGO RECORD.

PEAS AND LETTUCE.

Use a pint of peas and two young lettuces cut small. Put in as little water as possible to use and not burn, let them boil until tender, then add a square of sugar, the yolks of two eggs well beaten and two tablespoonfuls of cream. Stir together a short time but do not boil.

PEAS AU PARMESAN.

Grate one and one-half ounces of cheese, add to it two tablespoonfuls of cream, a gill of milk, a tablespoonful of butter, saltspoonful of salt and four shakes of pepper. Place in an enameled pan and stir over the fire until the butter and cheese are dissolved. Then put in a pint and a half of fresh young peas, previously boiled until tender, drained and seasoned with a half-teaspoonful of salt. Stir the mixture a few moments. Serve as hot as possible.

CHICAGO RECORD.

GREEN-PEA SALAD.

Shred some lettuce and add to it the peas—they should be boiled with a little mint, and be quite cold. Add the salad dressing just before serving.

PEA AND NUT SALAD.

Use one cupful of chopped pecan nuts to three cupfuls of French peas. Serve on lettuce with mayonnaise.

PEA SOUP.

Use chicken, mutton, or beef broth, or water for a liquor in which to boil two cups of green peas, add to them one minced onion, one carrot cut fine, a teaspoonful of chopped parsley, a stalk of celery cut fine, a bay leaf and two cloves. When the peas are tender, rub all through a sieve. Return the soup to the pot and add two tablespoonfuls of butter, a teaspoonful of salt, two well beaten yolks and half a cupful of cream. Let come to a boil and serve with croutons. Croutons are little squares of bread hard baked in the oven, or fried in oil or butter.

DEVILED PEPPERS.

Use green bell peppers, cut off the stem end and remove the inside. Chop cooked cold ham, and with it as many eggs as one wishes, or chop tongue, veal or chicken, and use the following salad dressing:—To a pint of meat use the yolk of a hard boiled egg, rubbed smooth in a scant tablespoonful of melted butter, a half teaspoonful of made mustard, half a teaspoonful of sugar, add enough vinegar to make it thin and stir in the meat. Fill the pepper shells with this mixture rounding it up high. It is an excellent lunch dish.

PEPPER MANGOES.

See Mangoes.

PICKLED PEPPERS.

Remove the seeds from large green peppers, slice them and lay them in a jar alternating each layer of peppers with a layer of cabbage, then cover them with salt and let stand over night. In the morning drain off the water. For the pickle use enough vinegar to cover the peppers, an ounce each of black and white mustard seed, juniper berries, whole cloves and allspice, one half-ounce of celery seed and one large onion chopped fine or one head of garlic if that flavor is liked. Let this come to a boil and pour over the peppers. Pack tightly in a jar, cover with horse-radish leaves, and close up tightly.

PEPPER SALAD.

Shave as fine as possible one head of cabbage, use an ounce of mustard seed, or an ounce of celery seed as one prefers either flavor; cut one or two yellow peppers into thin shavings if mustard seed is used, or four if celery seed is used. Pour cold cider vinegar over all, add a little salt and sugar and let stand a day or two to really pickle the cabbage and peppers. Pack in jars or cans and it will keep all winter. Serve with oysters and cold meats.

STUFFED PEPPERS.

Cut off the stem end of green bell peppers. Mince cooked chicken or use a can of shrimps, and mix with it almost an equal weight of bread crumbs, a large lump of butter, two or three tablespoonfuls of cream, salt and a sprinkle of parsley. Fill the pepper shells with the mixture, sprinkle bread crumbs over the tops, dot with butter, and brown in the oven.

OAKLAND STUFFED PEPPERS.

Cut off the tops and scoop out the seeds of six peppers, chop an extra pepper without seeds, mix with it a small onion chopped, a cupful of chopped tomato, two tablespoonfuls of butter or salad oil, a teaspoonful of salt, and an equal measure of bread crumbs. Stuff the peppers, replace the stem ends, and bake the peppers for half an hour, basting them with butter or salad oil two or three times. Serve them hot as a vegetable.

BROWNED MASHED POTATOES.

Whip up mashed potatoes with an egg-beater, add a few tablespoonfuls of cream, the yolks of two eggs, a tablespoonful of butter, pepper and salt. Cover with the whipped whites of the two eggs, bake until browned and with a pancake knife transfer them to a hot dish and serve at once.

POTATOES WITH CHEESE SAUCE.

Use twelve good sized potatoes, mash, add pepper, salt, milk and butter. Make a cup of drawn butter, (milk, butter and a very little corn starch as thickening, with pepper and salt) into it stir two beaten eggs, and two tablespoonfuls of grated cheese. Put a layer of potatoes on a pie tin, cover with a thin layer of the drawn butter sauce, cover this in turn with more potato and repeat until there is a mound, cover with the sauce, strew thickly with cheese and brown in a quick oven.

LYONNAISE POTATOES.

Put a large lump of butter in a saucepan and let it melt; then add one small onion chopped fine or sliced thin, when it is nicely browned but not scorched, put in slices of cold boiled potatoes, salt and pepper and cook until well browned. Just before taking up add a teaspoonful of parsley.

POTATO PANCAKES.

Grate eight large pared potatoes, add to them one and one half-teacupfuls of milk, the beaten yolks of two or three eggs, a lump of butter the size of a walnut, pepper, salt, enough flour to make a batter, and lastly add the whites of two or three eggs beaten stiff. Add a heaping teaspoonful of baking powder if only one egg is used. Fry in butter or drippings to a rich brown.

RINGED POTATOES.

Peel large potatoes, cut them round and round as one pares an apple, fry in clean, sweet, very hot lard until brown; drain on a sieve, sprinkle salt over them and serve.

POTATO TURNOVERS.

Use ten tablespoonfuls of whipped mashed potatoes with a little salt added gradually, six tablespoonfuls of flour and three tablespoonfuls of butter. When thoroughly mixed lay the mass upon a floured board and roll out about an inch thick, cut in circles with a small bowl, lay upon each circle minced meat, poultry or fish. Season the meat, wet the edges of the circle with beaten egg and close each one like a turnover, pinch them around the edges and fry to a light brown, or brush them with egg and brown them in the oven.

POTATO SOUFFLE.

Choose large, smooth, handsome, uniform potatoes, allow an extra potato for any waste. Bake and with a very sharp knife cut them in two lengthwise. Remove the inside, season with butter, cream, pepper and salt and fill the potato skins with the mixture; glaze them with the beaten whites of eggs and over the top spread the whites of eggs beaten to a stiff froth. Brown in the oven.

POTATO SOUP.

Use the water in which the potatoes were boiled, add three tablespoonfuls of mashed potato to a pint of water, and as much rich milk as there is water used, season with salt and a dust of cayenne pepper, a little juice of lemon or a little minced parsley or tarragon. Serve with crackers or croutons.

STUFFED POTATOES.

Bake handsome, uniform potatoes, cut off the tops with a sharp knife, take out the inside. Add to the scraped potato, butter, milk, pepper, salt and a little grated cheese, fill the empty shells and heap above the top. Grate a little cheese over this and set in the oven to brown. Serve hot.

POTATOES USED TO CLEANSE.

Small pieces of raw potato in a little water shaken vigorously inside bottles and lamp chimneys will clean them admirably. To clean a burned porcelain kettle boil peeled potatoes in it. Cold boiled potatoes not over-boiled, used as soap will clean the hands and keep them soft and healthy. To cleanse and stiffen silk, woolen and cotton fabrics use the following recipe:—Grate two good sized potatoes into a pint of clear, clean, soft water. Strain through a coarse sieve into a gallon of water and let the liquid settle. Pour the starchy fluid from the sediment, rub the articles gently in the liquid, rinse them thoroughly in clear water and then dry and press. Water in which potatoes are boiled is said to be very effective in keeping silver bright.

BAKED PUMPKIN.

Slice the pumpkin a quarter of an inch thick, peel and put a layer in the bottom of a baking dish, then a layer of sugar with a sprinkle of cinnamon and dot with butter, repeat this until the pan is full. Let the top be well covered with sugar. Bake in a moderate oven until the sugar becomes like a thick syrup. Or cut the pumpkin in squares and do not peel, bake, and when soft enough, scrape it from the shells, season with butter and salt and serve like squash.

CANNED PUMPKIN.

Stew pumpkin as for pies, put while hot in cans and seal.

PUMPKIN LOAF.

Take one quart of stewed pumpkin mashed fine, one teaspoonful each of salt and baking soda, one tablespoonful sugar, three pints of meal. Stir all together while boiling hot; steam four hours, or steam three hours and bake one. To be eaten hot with cream, or butter and sugar.

PUMPKIN MARMALADE.

Take ripe yellow pumpkins, pare and cut them into large pieces, scrape out the seed, weigh and to every pound take a pound of sugar and an orange or lemon. Grate the pieces of pumpkin on a coarse grater and put in the preserving kettle with sugar, the orange rind grated and the juice strained. Let it boil slowly, stirring frequently and skimming it well until it forms a smooth, thick marmalade. Put it warm into small glass jars or tumblers and when cold cover with a paper dipped in alcohol and another heavy paper pasted over the top of the glass.

PUMPKIN PIE.

To one quart of rich milk take three eggs, three big tablespoonfuls of sugar, a little salt, and a tablespoonful of ginger, a teaspoonful of cinnamon and a grated nutmeg if one likes it highly spiced, add enough finely stewed pumpkin to make a thin mixture. This will make three pies. A good pumpkin pie will puff up lightly when done.

PRESERVING PUMPKINS FOR WINTER USE.

A good way to prepare pumpkin for winter use is to cook and sift it as fine as for pies, then add nearly as much sugar as there is pumpkin; stir well and pack in crocks. Better than dried pumpkin for winter use.

PUMPKIN SOUP.

For six persons use three pounds of pumpkin; take off the rind, cut in pieces and put in a saucepan with a little salt and cover with water; let it boil until it is soft (about twenty minutes) and pass through a colander; it must have no water in it; put about three pints of milk in a saucepan, add the strained pumpkin, and let come to a boil; add a very little white sugar, some salt and pepper, but no butter. Serve hot.

HOW TO SERVE RADISHES.

Let every housekeeper try serving radishes in this dainty way. Cut off the root close to the radish and remove the leaves, leaving about an inch of the stem. Then cut the skin of the radish from the root toward the stem, in sections, as is done in removing the skin of an orange in eighths. The skin can then be peeled carefully back to the stem by slipping the point of a knife under it, and pulling it gently away from the heart of the radish. The pure white heart, with the soft pink of the peeling and the green stem makes a beautiful contrast. If they are thrown into cold water as fast as they are prepared and allowed to remain there until the time for serving, they will be much improved, becoming very crisp and tender. The skin of the young radish should never be discarded, as it contains properties of the vegetable that should always be eaten with the heart; and, unless the radish is tough, it will agree with a delicate stomach much better when eaten with the peel on. They look very dainty when served in this way, lying on fresh lettuce leaves, or are beautiful to use with parsley as a garnish for cold meats.

RADISH, CUCUMBER AND TOMATO SALAD.

Slice a bunch of radishes, and a cucumber very thin, make a bed of cress or lettuce, over this slice three solid tomatoes, and cover with the cucumbers and radish. Pour over all a French or mayonnaise dressing.

BAKED RHUBARB.

Peel rhubarb stalks, cut into inch lengths, put into a small stone crock with at least one part sugar to two parts fruit, or a larger part if liked, but not one particle of water, bake until the pieces are clear; flavor with lemon or it is good without. It is a prettier sauce and takes less sugar than when stewed, and can be used for a pie filling if the crust is made first. To prevent burning, the crock may be set in a pan of boiling water. When done and while yet hot, beat up the whites of two eggs and whip into the sauce. It makes it very light and very nice.

BOTTLED RHUBARB.

Use perfectly fresh, crisp rhubarb, peel and cut in small pieces as for pies, fill a Mason jar with the fruit and pour over it freshly drawn water. Screw on the top and by the next morning the water will have settled in the jar. Fill the jars full with fresh water, seal again and the fruit is ready for winter's use. In making pies it takes less sugar than the fresh fruit. Or, boil the rhubarb a few moments, as for sauce, with or without sugar and put into jars while it is very hot just as other fruit is canned.

RHUBARB COBBLER.

Two cups of flour sifted with two teaspoons of baking powder and one-half teaspoon of salt. Rub in two tablespoons of butter. Beat one egg very light and add it to three-fourths of a cup of milk. Mix with the other ingredients, line the sides of a baking dish with this crust. Take one quart of chopped rhubarb sweetened with three cups of sugar, fill the pudding dish with the rhubarb; roll out the remaining crust, cover the top of dish and bake one-half hour.

Mrs. Laura Whitehead.

CREAM RHUBARB PIE.

One cup of rhubarb which has been peeled and chopped fine; add one cup of sugar and the grated rind of a lemon. In a teacup place one tablespoonful of corn-starch and moisten it with as much cold water; fill up the cup with boiling water and add it to the rhubarb. Add the yolks of three eggs well beaten. Bake with an under crust. When cold cover with a meringue made of the whites of the eggs and one-half cup of sugar. Place in the oven to become a delicate brown. Very fine.

Mrs. Byron Backus.

RHUBARB JAM.

Use equal parts of rhubarb and sugar, heat the sugar with as little water as will keep it from burning, pour over the rhubarb and let stand several hours; pour off and boil until it thickens, then add the fruit and boil gently for fifteen minutes. Put up in jelly glasses. Apples and oranges may be put up with rhubarb allowing two apples or three oranges to a pint of cut up rhubarb.

RHUBARB TAPIOCA.

Soak over night two-thirds of a cupful of tapioca. In the morning drain; add one cupful of water and cook the tapioca until it is clear; add a little more water if necessary. Then add a cup and a half of finely sliced rhubarb, a pinch of salt and a large half-cup of sugar. Bake in moderate oven an hour. Serve warm or cold and eat with sugar if liked very sweet. Very nice.

Shirley De Forest.

RUTABAGAS BOILED.

Pare, slice and boil in as little salted water as possible, a little sugar added is an improvement. When dry and tender serve plain, each slice buttered and peppered as it is piled on the plate.

RUTABAGAS AND POTATOES.

Use three-fourths potatoes and one-fourth rutabagas; boil in salted water until tender, add a lump of butter, a dust of pepper and more salt if necessary, mash and stir until fine and light. Any good recipe for white turnips is equally good for rutabagas.

SALAD DRESSINGS.

Cream Dressing.—Where oil is disliked in salads, the following dressing will be found excellent. Rub the yolks of two hard-boiled eggs very fine with a spoon, incorporate with them a dessertspoonful of mixed mustard, then stir in a tablespoonful of melted butter, half a teacupful of thick cream, a saltspoonful of salt, and cayenne pepper enough to take up on the point of a very small pen-knife blade, and a few drops of anchovy or Worcestershire sauce; add very carefully sufficient vinegar to reduce the mixture to a smooth, creamy consistency.

French Dressing.—Use one tablespoonful of vinegar to three of salad oil (melted butter will do) one teaspoonful of salt to half the quantity of pepper and a teaspoonful of made mustard. Mix the salt, pepper, mustard and oil together, then add the vinegar a few drops at a time, stirring fast. A teaspoonful of scraped onion may be added for those who like the flavor.

Mayonnaise Dressing.—Put in the bottom of a quart bowl the yolk of a raw egg, a level teaspoonful of salt, and three-fourths of a teaspoonful of pepper; have ready about half a cupful of vinegar, and a bottle of salad oil; use a wooden spoon and fork for mixing the mayonnaise—first the egg and seasoning together, then begin to add the oil, two or three drops at a time, stirring the mayonnaise constantly until a thick paste is formed; to this add two or three drops at a time, still stirring, enough vinegar to reduce the paste to the consistency of thick cream; then stir in more oil, until the mayonnaise is again stiff, when a little more vinegar should be added; proceed in this way until the oil is all used, being careful toward the last to use the vinegar cautiously, so that when the mayonnaise is finished it will be stiff enough to remain on the top of the salad. Some like the addition of a level teaspoonful of dry mustard to a pint of mayonnaise.

Plain Salad Dressing.—Set a bowl over a boiling teakettle, into it put a table-spoonful each of melted butter and mustard, rub them well together, then add a tablespoonful of sugar, one half-cup of vinegar and lastly three well-beaten eggs. Stir constantly while cooking, to make the mixture smooth, when done, strain and bottle for use. If too thick upon serving, thin with cream.

BOILED SALSIFY.

Scrape off the outer skin of the roots, cut in small pieces and throw into water with a little vinegar to prevent turning brown. Boil at least an hour, as they should be quite soft to be good. When done put in a little salt codfish picked very fine. Season with butter, salt, and cream, thickened with a little flour or cornstarch and serve with bits of toast. The fish helps to give it a sea-flavor. Instead of fish the juice of half a lemon may be used or it is good without any added flavor.

ESCALLOPED SALSIFY.

Cook salsify in salted water until tender, alternate it in a baking dish with bread crumbs seasoned with pepper and salt, and dot with butter. Moisten it with cream or milk and a little melted butter, cover the top with bread crumbs dotted with butter, and bake a light brown.

SALSIFY FRITTERS.

Scrape some oyster plant and drop quickly into cold water with a few drops of vinegar to prevent its turning dark. Boil until soft in salted water, mash fine, and for every half pint of the pulp add one well beaten egg, a teaspoonful of melted butter, a tablespoonful of cream, a heaping tablespoonful of flour, salt and pepper. Drop into boiling lard or drippings and fry brown. Or, instead of mashing the salsify after boiling, some prefer to drain it, and to dip each piece in batter and fry it in hot lard. Season with salt and pepper after frying, drain in a napkin and serve hot.

FRIED SALSIFY.

Scrape, cut into finger lengths and boil in salted water, drain and cover with a dressing of oil and vinegar, salt and pepper. Let stand until well seasoned, then drain again, sprinkle with parsley and fry in hot fat. Put in but few pieces at a time as each needs attention. Dry in a hot colander and serve.

SALSIFY SOUP.

Use a pint of salsify cut fine, boil until soft in a pint of water, mash and put through a sieve. Have ready three pints of boiling milk, into this put the salsify, liquor and pulp, thicken with a tablespoonful of flour, and season with butter, pepper and salt. Roll crackers and stir in three tablespoonfuls of cracker dust.

SAUCES.

Asparagus Sauce.—Use the tender part of the stalks for the main dish, boil the tougher part until it is as soft as it will be, then rub through a coarse sieve. Put the pulp into a mixture of one tablespoonful each of butter and flour and let it simmer for a few moments, add a half-cup of water in which the asparagus was boiled, season with salt and pepper and boil thoroughly; just before taking from the fire add a half-cup of hot cream or one-half cup of milk and water, and a teaspoonful of butter; a little grating of nutmeg improves the flavor.

Bechamel Sauce.—Bechamel sauce is a white one and needs a white stock; if there is none at hand make it in the following manner: cut up lean veal, free from fat into three-inch cubes and put them into a stewpan. Add one small onion, one small carrot cut into pieces, and six ounces of butter. Fry the vegetables in the butter ten minutes, without coloring, then stir in three ounces of flour, and continue stirring five minutes longer. Add three pints of stock, one pint of cream, five ounces of mushrooms, a small sprinkling of dried herbs, one half teaspoonful of salt and a pinch of white pepper. Stir until it comes to a boil, skim occasionally to remove the fat, and simmer for two hours. Strain through a cloth or fine sieve into a porcelain stewpan with a gill of cream. Simmer over the fire till it coats the spoon, strain again through a cloth or fine sieve into a basin, and set till the sauce is cold. This sauce requires the cook's utmost attention.

Butter Sauce or Drawn Butter Sauce.—Mix one tablespoonful each of butter and flour to a smooth paste, put in a saucepan to melt, not to brown, and add one cupful of water, broth, or milk. Season with one teaspoonful of salt and one saltspoonful of pepper. Stir constantly while boiling. This is a good sauce in itself and is the foundation of many other sauces; it is varied with different vegetable flavors, catsups, vinegars, spices, lemon juice, leaves and the different sweet herbs.

Brown Sauce or Spanish Sauce.—Brown a tablespoonful of butter, add the same amount of flour and brown again, add a cup of boiling water, stock or milk, and stir while it is cooking, strain if necessary; a clove, a bay leaf, and a tablespoon-ful of minced onion or carrot browned in the butter varies the flavor.

Caper Sauce.—Stir into some good melted butter from three to four des-sertspoonfuls of capers; add a little of the vinegar and dish the sauce as soon as it boils.

Celery Sauce.—Cut half a dozen heads, or so, of celery into small pieces; cook in a little slightly salted water until tender, and then rub through a colander. Put a pint of white stock into a stewpan with two blades of mace, and a small bunch of savory herbs; simmer half an hour to extract their flavor, then strain them out, add the celery and a thickening of flour or corn-starch; scald well, and just before serv-ing, pour in a teacupful of cream, or if one has not the cream, use the same amount of scalded milk and a tablespoonful of butter, season to taste with salt and white pepper, squeeze in a little lemon juice, if one has it, and serve. If brown gravy is preferred thicken with browned flour, and it is improved by a little Worcestershire sauce or mushroom catsup.

Cream Sauce.—Rub to a smooth paste one tablespoonful of butter and the same of flour, put into a saucepan and melt, do not brown; have ready a cup of hot cream, or the same amount of milk enriched by a tablespoonful of butter and add to the butter and flour. Stir constantly until it thickens. A dusting of grated nutmeg, grated cheese or a saltspoonful of chopped onion lightly browned in the butter is an agreeable addition.

Cucumber Sauce.—Use two tablespoonfuls of olive oil, a scant tablespoonful of vinegar or lemon juice, a half-teaspoonful of salt, a dash of pepper, and a saltspoonful of mustard with a teaspoonful of cucumber; rub the oil and mustard together before adding the other ingredients, stir well and serve very soon as it spoils by standing.

Egg Sauce.—Boil the eggs hard, cut them into small squares, and mix them with good butter sauce. Make hot and add a little lemon juice before serving.

Hollandaise Sauce.—One half a teacupful of butter, the juice of half a lemon, the yolks of two eggs, a speck of cayenne, one-half cupful of boiling water, one-half teaspoonful of salt; beat the butter to a cream, add the yolks one by one, the lemon juice, pepper and salt; place the bowl in which these are mixed in a saucepan of boiling water; beat with an egg-beater until the sauce begins to thicken, and add boiling water, beating all the time; when like a soft custard, it is done; the bowl, if thin, must be kept over the fire not more than five minutes, as if boiled too much it spoils.

Horseradish Sauce.—Two teaspoonfuls of made mustard, two of white sugar, one-half teaspoonful of salt and a gill of vinegar; mix and pour over sufficient grated horseradish to moisten thoroughly.

Lyonnaise Sauce.—Brown a small onion minced in a tablespoonful of butter and the same of flour, add a half-cupful of meat broth, a teaspoonful of parsley, salt and pepper and cook long enough to season well.

Mint Sauce.—Four dessertspoonfuls of mint, two of sugar, one gill of vinegar; stir all together; make two or three hours before wanted.

Mushroom Sauce.—Mix one tablespoonful each of flour and butter, melt in a stewpan, add a cupful of rich white stock or cream and stir until it thickens; put in a half-cupful of freshly boiled or of canned mushrooms, let all come to a boil again, season with a saltspoonful of salt and a dash of cayenne pepper; serve hot.

Mustard Sauce, French.—Slice an onion in a bowl; cover with good vinegar. After two days pour off the vinegar; add to it a teaspoonful of cayenne pepper, a teaspoonful of salt, a tablespoonful of sugar, and mustard enough to thicken; mix, set upon the stove and stir until it boils. When cold it is ready for use.

Mustard Sauce, German.—Four tablespoonfuls of ground mustard, one tablespoonful of flour, two teaspoonfuls of sugar, one of salt, two of cinnamon, one of cloves, one of cayenne pepper, three of melted butter; mix with one pint of boiling vinegar.

Onion Sauce.—Mince an onion; fry it in butter in a stewpan. Pour over it a gill of vinegar; let it remain on the stove until it is simmered one-third away. Add a pint of gravy, a bunch of parsley, two or three cloves, pepper and salt. Thicken with a little flour and butter, strain, and remove any particles of fat.

Parsley Sauce.—Parsley sauce is the usual "cream sauce," to which is added a tablespoonful of minced parsley and one hard boiled egg finely chopped.

Tartare Sauce.—Tartare sauce is a French salad dressing to which is added a tablespoonful each of chopped olives, parsley, and capers or nasturtiums; instead of capers or nasturtiums chopped cucumbers or gherkins can be used. Set on ice until used.

Tomato Sauce.—Boil together for one hour, a pint of tomatoes, one gill of broth of any kind, one sprig of thyme, three whole cloves, three pepper corns, and half an ounce of sliced onions; rub through a sieve with a wooden spoon, and set the sauce to keep hot; mix together over the fire one ounce of butter and half an ounce of flour, and when smooth add to the tomato sauce.

Vinaigrette Sauce.—A vinaigrette sauce is a brown sauce flavored with vinegar just before serving; it must be cider vinegar, or one of the fancy vinegars, as tarragon, parsley, martynia and the like; or, rub a teaspoonful of mustard into a tablespoonful of olive oil, to which add a teaspoonful of salt and one-half teaspoonful of pepper. Lastly add very slowly a half-cup of vinegar stirring vigorously.

White Sauce.—Put one tablespoon each of flour and butter in a saucepan and stir together until they bubble; then gradually stir in a pint of boiling water or white stock; season with salt and pepper and let boil a moment longer. To vary it, the beaten whites of two eggs may be stirred in just before serving.

SCORZONERA.

The roots are eaten boiled like those of salsify—or like the Jerusalem artichoke. The recipes of either are applicable to scorzonera. The leaves of scorzonera are used in salad with a plain or French dressing.

SHALLOTS.

The bulbs are more delicate than onions, and are used to flavor soups, salads, dressings and sauces. The leaves when young help in forming salads.

SORREL AND SWISS CHARD.

Sorrel and Swiss chard are often used together as the chard modifies the acidity of the sorrel. They make acceptable greens when used together and are treated like spinach.

SORREL SOUP.

Pick off the stems and wash the leaves of a quart of sorrel, boil in salted water, drain and chop fine, mix butter and flour in a saucepan and when the butter is melted turn in the sorrel and let cook for a couple of minutes. Add three pints of beef or veal stock well seasoned and stir until it boils. Just before serving beat up two eggs and turn over them the boiling soup, which will cook them sufficiently. A sliced onion, or a few blades of chives boiled with the sorrel is a welcome flavor occasionally, also the stock may be half meat stock and half cream or milk.

SORREL AND SPINACH SOUP.

To one quart of sorrel add a handful of spinach and a few lettuce leaves. Put them in a frying pan with a large piece of butter and cook until done. Add two quarts of boiling water, season with salt and pepper and just before serving add two eggs well beaten into a gill of cream. This is an excellent soup for an invalid.

BAKED SPINACH.

Use one-half peck of spinach. Pick over the leaves carefully, remove all wilted ones and roots, wash thoroughly and put in boiling water to which a pinch of soda has been added to keep the color. When very tender, drain, chop fine, and put into a baking dish. Put into a saucepan with a cup of milk, a tablespoonful of butter, one small teaspoonful of salt, a dash of cayenne pepper and a very little grated nutmeg. Let this come to a boil, stir into the spinach, add two well beaten eggs and bake ten minutes in a hot oven.

BOILED SPINACH, FRENCH.

Prepare as above, after it is thoroughly tender, throw into a colander and drench with cold water. This gives a firmness and delicacy attained in no other way. Shake it free from water, chop fine, put into a saucepan, stir with a tablespoonful of butter, salt and pepper to taste and two tablespoonfuls of cream until hot, when it is ready to be heaped in the dish with poached or boiled eggs or quirled yolks on top. To quirl the yolks run them through the sieve of a patent potato masher.

"VICTORY" SPINACH

Carefully wash the spinach, scald it in boiling salted water, then pour cold water over it, drain and chop fine. Stew an onion in butter until it is soft, add the spinach, sprinkle flour over it and cook for ten minutes stirring constantly, add salt, pepper, a little grated nutmeg, and cover with meat stock or gravy. Boil a few minutes and when done, add a little sour cream.

FRIED SPINACH.

Take cold spinach left from dinner, premising that it was boiled tender in properly salted water, and that there were three or four poached eggs left also. Chop the eggs thoroughly into the spinach and sprinkle with pepper. Put into a frying-pan a large tablespoonful of butter, and when it is sufficiently hot put in the spinach and eggs, and fry nicely.

RAVIOLI OF SPINACH.

Prepare a potato paste as for Potato Turnovers, or a good puff paste, and with a saucer or tin cutter of that size cut out a circle. Place a tablespoonful of spinach prepared French style upon one side, wet the edges, fold over the other side and press it around with the fingers and thumb, brush with egg and bake until a light brown. When served pour around it cream or a cream sauce in which is a hard boiled egg chopped fine, or peas.

SPINACH SALAD.

Take two dozen heads of spinach, season with salt and pepper, put in salad dish and set away on ice. Take the yolks of three hard boiled eggs, mash fine, add mustard, salt, pepper, a tablespoonful of melted butter. Mix thoroughly, add vinegar and pour over the spinach. Garnish with hard boiled eggs sliced.

COOKING SUMMER SQUASH.

Quarter, seed, pare and lay them in cold water. Steam over boiling soft water if possible, or boil in salted water and drain thoroughly, mash them smooth and season with butter, pepper and salt. If the seeds are very young and tender they can be retained.

ESCALLOPED SUMMER SQUASH.

The squash is pared and sliced and laid in a baking dish alternating with cracker crumbs, seasoned with butter, pepper and salt, until the dish is full, the upper layer being cracker crumbs dotted with butter. Bake three quarters of an hour.

FRIED SUMMER SQUASH.

Cut the squash in thin slices and sprinkle with salt. Let it stand a few minutes, then beat an egg, in which dip the slices. Fry in butter and season with sugar or salt and pepper to taste.

SUMMER SQUASH FRITTERS.

Use three medium sized squashes; pare, cut up and boil tender, drain thoroughly and mash, season with pepper and salt; add one cupful of milk (cream is better), the yolks of two eggs and sufficient sifted flour to make a very stiff batter, or they will be hard to turn; lastly, stir in the beaten whites of the eggs. Fry brown in hot fat.

BAKED WINTER SQUASH.

Cut in small pieces to serve individually, bake with the rind on, scoop out the squash, season it with butter, pepper, salt, a little sugar and cream and replace in shells; an allowance of two or three extra pieces should be made to give filling enough to heap the shells, dust a few bread or cracker crumbs over the top, dot with a bit of butter, bake a nice brown and serve.

BOILED WINTER SQUASH.

Peel and cut into pieces a large squash that will, when cooked fill a half gallon. Steam over hot salted water if possible, if not put it on to boil in as little water as possible. Keep it closely covered and stir frequently. When perfectly soft, drain in colander, press out all of the water, rub the squash through a sieve and return it to the saucepan. Add to it a quarter of a pound of nice butter, one gill of sweet cream and salt and pepper to taste. Stew slowly, stirring frequently until it is as dry as possible. In cold weather serve all vegetables on warmed dishes.

SQUASH BISCUIT.

One and one-half cupfuls of sifted squash, half a cupful of sugar, half a cake of compressed yeast, one cupful of milk, half a teaspoonful of salt, four tablespoonfuls of butter, five cupfuls of flour. Dissolve the yeast in a scant half-cupful of cold water, mix it and the milk, butter, salt, sugar and squash together, and stir into the flour. Knead well and let it rise over night. In the morning shape into biscuit. Let them rise one hour and a half and bake one hour.

Chicago Record.

SQUASH CUSTARD.

Use a cupful of mashed squash, stir into it a pint of hot milk, then add four well beaten eggs, a tablespoonful of butter, and season with salt and pepper. Put into a hot greased baking pan and bake in a quick oven.

SQUASH PIE.

See Pumpkin Pie.

SQUASH SOUP.

To one quart of thoroughly cooked pumpkin or squash allow two quarts of milk, plenty of butter, pepper and salt. Serve with toasted bread. Pumpkin and squash soups are French dishes.

SWEET POTATO BISCUIT.

One quart of flour, one quart of sweet potatoes—after they are boiled and grated—one-half cupful of lard, one cup of yeast—mix with either milk or water; let them rise twice. Bake like tea biscuits.

ESCALLOPED SWEET POTATOES.

Boil the potatoes the day before. Peel and slice them rather thick. In the bottom of a baking-dish put bits of butter, sprinkle sugar and put a layer of potato. Then more butter, sugar and potato, until the pan is full. Let the top be strewn with sugar and bits of butter and pour over it a teacupful of water. Put it in the oven, and after it begins to cook, once or twice moisten the top with a little butter and water to dissolve the sugar and prevent its merely drying on top of the potato. Use a teacupful of sugar and half a pound of butter to a half gallon pan of potato. Bake slowly.

SWEET POTATO LOAF.

Boil and mash sweet potatoes, season with butter, pepper and salt, put into a buttered baking dish, cover with bread crumbs dotted with butter, and bake until brown. Ornament with cress or a few sprigs of parsley.

SWEET POTATOES ROASTED.

Sweet potatoes roasted under beef or lamb are very nice. Take the skin off carefully to leave the surface smooth, wash and put them under the meat, allowing half an hour for a medium sized potato. They will brown over nicely and receive an agreeable flavor.

SWEET POTATO SALAD.

Boil three large sweet potatoes. Cut into half-inch squares. Cut into very small pieces two stalks of celery. Season with salt and pepper and pour over a French dressing as follows:—Three tablespoonfuls salad oil, two of vinegar, one table-spoonful onion juice, one saltspoon each of salt and pepper. Let salad stand in refrigerator two hours. Garnish with pickles, pitted olives and parsley.

CHICAGO RECORD.

SWISS CHARD OR SILVER LEAF BEET.

The leaves of Swiss Chard are boiled and used like spinach. The stalks and midrib are very broad and tender and when young are used like asparagus. The leaves of sorrel and spinach are often used together as greens. (See **Asparagus** and **Spinach** receipts).

BAKED TOMATOES.

Tomatoes may be simply baked without stuffing. Peel them first, lay stem end down in a dripping pan, cut a Greek cross on the top of each, season with salt, pepper and sugar, dot with bits of butter and sprinkle thickly with fine stale crumbs, adding a generous bit of butter on top of each. Pour in at the side of the pan two tablespoonfuls of water.

BROILED TOMATOES.

Turn hot boiling water on to the tomatoes to peel them, cut slices at least three-quarters of an inch thick, and small tomatoes in halves, rub a piece of fat pork on the gridiron, put on the tomatoes, and broil on both sides, or dip in sweet oil and broil, or cover both sides with cheese and broil, or slice the tomatoes with their skins on and broil, and pour melted butter over them. In all cases season nicely with salt and pepper, garnish with parsley or cress and serve hot on a hot dish.

ESCALLOPED TOMATOES.

Arrange in a baking pan layers of tomatoes covered with bread crumbs seasoned with salt, pepper, a little sugar, and dotted with butter. Let the upper layer be of bread crumbs dotted with butter. Bake covered, half an hour. A few minutes before serving take off the cover and brown.

TOMATO CATSUP.

Use ripe tomatoes, boil and strain. To every gallon of tomatoes use 3 tablespoonfuls of salt, 2 of mustard, 1 1/2 black pepper, 1/4 of cayenne, cup of brown sugar and 1 pint of cider vinegar. Boil four hours and watch carefully or it will burn. Set on back of stove and add 1 tablespoonful of cinnamon, 1/2 tablespoonful of cloves, and if liked, 1 pint currant jelly. Mix thoroughly, can while hot and seal.

TOMATO FIGS.

Scald and peel the tomatoes, then weigh them, place them in a stone jar with an equal amount of sugar and let them stand two days, then pour off the syrup and boil and skim until no scum rises. Pour it over the tomatoes and let them stand two days as before, pour off, boil and skim a second time and a third time. After the third time they are fit to dry if the weather is good, if not let them stand in syrup until drying weather. Place on earthen dishes and dry in the sun which will take about a week, after which pack them in wooden boxes with fine white paper between the layers; so prepared they will keep for years.

FRIED TOMATOES.

Do not pare the tomatoes, cut in slices, roll in flour and fry in butter until both sides are brown, season with salt, pepper and a little sugar sprinkled over while cooking; or after the tomatoes are browned, stir into the gravy in the spider, one cupful of cream thickened with flour. Let it boil up, and turn it over the tomatoes.

MACARONI WITH TOMATOES.

Remove from each tomato the pips and watery substance it contains; put the tomatoes in a saucepan with a small piece of butter, pepper, salt, thyme and a bay leaf, and a few tablespoonfuls of gravy or stock, keep stirring until they are reduced to a pulp, then strain through a sieve, and pour over macaroni already boiled soft and cover with grated cheese; bake until a light brown.

TOMATO MANGOES. (SEE MANGOES.)

TOMATO MUSTARD.

To one peck of ripe tomatoes add a teaspoonful of salt; let it stew a half hour, and strain through a sieve. Add two dessertspoonfuls of onions chopped fine, a dessertspoonful of whole pepper, one of allspice, one of cloves, and half a spoonful of cayenne pepper. Let it simmer down one-third, adding a teaspoonful of curry, and a teacupful of mustard. Then simmer half an hour longer.

FROZEN TOMATO SALAD.

Peel and chop fine a half dozen solid tomatoes, season with a teaspoonful of salt, a saltspoonful of pepper and a teaspoonful of lemon juice. Freeze the pulp solid in an ice cream freezer, when frozen mold it into fancy shapes and serve on lettuce with a tablespoonful of mayonnaise over each mold.

TOMATO SOUP.

Boil a quart of tomatoes in a pint of water for twenty minutes and strain; put in a small teaspoonful of soda, and a quart of milk as it foams. Add a tablespoonful of butter and two tablespoonfuls of cornstarch rubbed together, plenty of salt and a sprinkling of pepper. Put a tablespoonful of whipped cream in each soup plate.

STUFFED TOMATOES.

Cut off a transverse slice from the stem end of the tomato; scrape out the inside pulp and stuff it with mashed potatoes, bread crumbs, parsley and onions, or with any force meat, fish, or poultry well seasoned with butter, pepper and salt, moistened with a little stock or cream and the yolk of an egg added to bind it, bake. Or, scoop out the seeds, place the tomatoes in a saucepan containing a gill of salad oil; next chop about half a bottle of mushrooms, a handful of parsley and four shallots, put them into a stewpan with two ounces of scraped bacon or ham, season with pepper, salt, a little chopped thyme and fry five minutes, when add the yolks of three eggs. Fill the tomatoes with this mixture, sprinkle with bread crumbs and bake until brown.

TOMATO WINE.

Take fresh ripe tomatoes, mash very fine, strain through a thin cloth. To every gallon of the pure juice add one and one-quarter pounds of sugar and set away in an earthen jar about nine days or until it has fermented; a little salt will improve its taste; strain again, bottle, cork tightly and tie down cork. To use it as a drink, to every gallon of fresh sweetened water add half a tumbler of the wine with a few drops of lemon essence and one has a good substitute for lemonade.

KIZZIE BECKLY.

BAKED TURNIPS.

Peel and boil some turnips in salted water to which a half teaspoonful of sugar has been added. Slice them half an inch thick and put them in a stew-pan with two tablespoonfuls of butter to six or seven good sized turnips, shake them until they are lightly browned. Season with salt, pepper, a trifle of mace and sugar. Pour over a pint of good brown gravy and serve.

BOILED TURNIPS.

Put three tablespoonfuls of butter in a saucepan and as soon as it is melted put in one small onion, minced fine and one quart of turnips cut in dice; stir until they are brown, when add one teaspoonful of salt, the same of sugar, one tablespoonful of flour and half a saltspoonful of pepper, stirring for two minutes. Then add a cupful of milk or stock and simmer for twenty minutes, keeping the saucepan covered. Serve immediately.

TURNIP SALAD.

Slice very thin three or four turnips; put them to soak over night, change the water the next morning, then cut up very fine, put on salt, pepper, celery salt, or celery seed and vinegar.

VEGETABLE ASPIC MOLDS.

In the bottom of some very small molds lay alternately small pieces of chili, chervil and hard-boiled white of egg. Cover these well with liquid aspic, then add a further layer of chopped parsley and finely chopped yolk of hard-boiled egg. Having covered this also with aspic, put in another layer of small squares of cheese and a few capers, and so continue the operation till the molds are quite full. When set on ice turn out of the molds and serve on lettuce leaves with mustard, cress and chopped aspic jelly. The aspic is made by using a meat or vegetable stock to which is added enough soaked gelatine to make a jelly when cold.

VEGETABLE SOUP.

Put a half-cup of drippings into a saucepan, thicken it with two tablespoonfuls of flour, cut into it and brown two small onions. Have ready two quarts of boiling water, into this empty the contents of the saucepan, slice into it six tomatoes, two potatoes, one carrot and one turnip; add two cupfuls of green peas, one cupful of lima beans and a half-dozen cloves. Let all simmer slowly for two hours, then put all through a colander, return it to the pot, heat to boiling, thicken with a tablespoonful of butter rolled in cornstarch, season with pepper and salt to taste and serve hot.

Lector House believes that a society develops through a two-fold approach of continuous learning and adaptation, which is derived from the study of classic literary works spread across the historic timeline of literature records. Therefore, we aim at reviving, repairing and redeveloping all those inaccessible or damaged but historically as well as culturally important literature across subjects so that the future generations may have an opportunity to study and learn from past works to embark upon a journey of creating a better future.

This book is a result of an effort made by Lector House towards making a contribution to the preservation and repair of original ancient works which might hold historical significance to the approach of continuous learning across subjects.

HAPPY READING & LEARNING!

LECTOR HOUSE
LECTOR HOUSE LLP
E-MAIL: lectorpublishing@gmail.com

www.ingramcontent.com/pod-product-compliance
Lightning Source LLC
Chambersburg PA
CBHW051451140726
47987CB00006B/2656